CANYON COUNTRY
Wildflowers

A FIELD GUIDE TO
COMMON WILDFLOWERS, SHRUBS,
AND TREES

Text by Damian Fagan
Photos by Damian Fagan and others

FALCON®

Falcon® Publishing Co., Inc., Helena and Billings, Montana

Published in cooperation with **the Canyonlands Natural History Association.**

DEDICATION

To my two favorite desert wildflowers—Raven and Luna—
and to Thom Newcomb, who introduced me to the oaks
and pines of my youth.

All inside illustrations and background cover illustration by DD Dowden.
Front and back cover photos by Damian Fagan.

© 1998 by Falcon® Publishing Co., Inc.,
Helena and Billings, Montana.

Published in cooperation with the Canyonlands Natural History Association.

10 9 8 7 6 5 4 3 2

Editing, design, typesetting, and other prepress work by Falcon, Helena, Montana.
Printing in Hong Kong.

Library of Congress Cataloging-in-Publication data:
Fagan, Damian.
     Canyon country wildflowers : a field guide to common wildflowers,
     shrubs, and trees / text and photos by Damian Fagan.
         p.   cm.
     Includes bibliographical references (p.   ) and index.
     ISBN 1-56044-560-2 (pbk.)
         1. Wild flowers—Utah—Canyonlands National Park Region—
     Identification. 2. Shrubs—Utah—Canyonlands National Park Region—
     Identification. 3. Trees—Utah—Canyonlands National Park Region—
     Identification. 4. Wild flowers—Utah—Canyonlands National Park
     Region—Pictorial works. 5. Shrubs—Utah—Canyonlands National Park
     Region—Pictorial works. 6. Trees—Utah—Canyonlands National Park
     Region—Pictorial works.   I. Title.
     QK189.F34 1998
     582.13'09792'59—dc21   97-31824
                                                            CIP

For extra copies of this book please check with your local bookstore,
or write Falcon, P.O. Box 1718, Helena, MT 59624.
You may also call toll-free 1-800-582-2665, or to contact us via e-mail, visit our homepage
on the world wide web at http://www.falconguide.com.

$\mathcal{C}$ONTENTS

PREFACE

It was another Friday night in Moab. Downtown was active as the restaurants, shops, motels, and bars filled with patrons. But instead of heading for the neon glow and bustle of the eateries, five of us, plus our dogs, drove up to the Sand Flats area near "the world's most scenic dump." We were on a pilgrimage of sorts; we searched for *Oenothera pallida,* the Pale Evening-Primrose. When we found one ripe with floral buds, we sat down around the plant like expecting parents and waited—and watched. Slowly, oh so slowly, a flower bud unraveled, the tight sepals giving way as the petals burst forth for the grand finale. The whole process took about twenty minutes, fast enough to see and slow enough to absorb the unfolding drama. We joked about Friday nights in Moab and what the locals do for fun.

This night gave me a greater appreciation for flowers; having considered the amount of energy expended to produce one flower, I rarely pick flowers anymore. The event also encouraged me to "experience" these plants to a greater depth, to go beyond the nomenclature and really look at the plant in all its complexity. To get down on my knees in the soft dirt or the rough gravel and inhale the flower's fragrance. To invert binoculars for a makeshift hand lens and search the flower for pollinators and even predators such as crab spiders that lurk among the blossoms. To remember that we are nature, and nature *does* matter. To put aside science and facts and a system of Latin names and just sit and watch and wait for nature to unravel itself in the simple, yet elegant, form of a desert wildflower.

ACKNOWLEDGMENTS

Thanks to Megan Hiller and Bill Schneider of Falcon Publishing for the opportunity to write this book and for their support during the project. Thanks also to Gloria Brown for her encouragement. I appreciate the Canyonlands Natural History Association for its continued support as well. Thanks to Julie Schroeder, a copyeditor whose botanical knowledge made this a better book. My wife Raven and I spent many years learning about the plants of the Canyonlands region while we were employed by the National Park Service; her enthusiasm about plants kept me interested, even when I switched to watching birds. I am indebted to Joel Tuhy of the Moab office of The Nature Conservancy and Sonja Nicolaison, a national park ranger, for their assistance in species identification. I would also like to thank David Williams, Tara Williams, and Linda Whitham for information, ideas, and identification of several species. The National Park Service Southeast Utah Group allowed me time in its herbarium for which I am grateful. Thanks go to Diane Allen, Joel Tuhy, Andrea Brand, Dan McRoberts, Judie Chrobak-Cox, Gary Salamacha, and Raven Tennyson for submitting photographs and answering queries. And to my daughter Luna, special gratitude—she, at almost-two, has brought me to her level of seeing plants, nose to flower. And to the flowers themselves, which have brought me hours of joy and wonderment: long may you bloom.

COLORADO PLATEAU AND
CANYONLANDS REGION

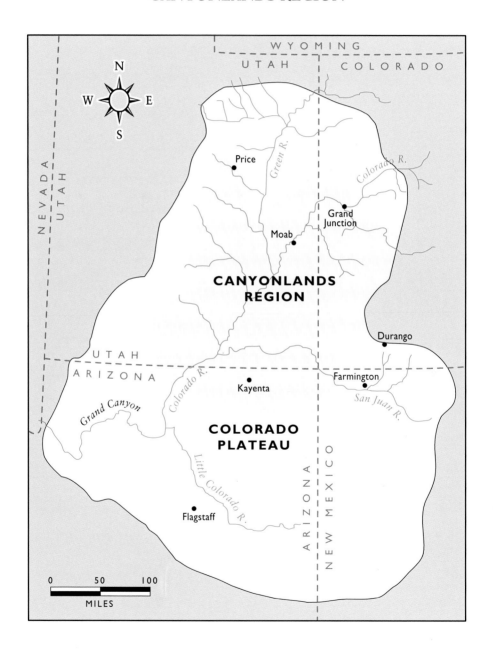

WYOMING

UTAH · COLORADO

N
W · E
S

NEVADA | UTAH

Price

Green R.

Colorado R.

Grand
Junction

Moab

CANYONLANDS
REGION

Durango

UTAH
ARIZONA

Colorado R.

Kayenta

Farmington

San Juan R.

Grand Canyon

COLORADO
PLATEAU

Little Colorado R.

ARIZONA | NEW MEXICO

Flagstaff

0   50   100
MILES

INTRODUCTION

The Colorado Plateau and Canyonlands Region

The Colorado Plateau is a unique geographical area that encompasses approximately 133,000 square miles and stretches over portions of Utah, Colorado, New Mexico, and Arizona. Defined by thick accumulations of sedimentary deposits, a semiarid climate, relatively high elevation, sparse vegetation, isolated mountain ranges, and vast areas of open sandstone, this landscape is world-renowned for its angular topography of deep canyons, massive cliffs, and steplike escarpments.

The Canyonlands region is in the center of the Colorado Plateau; it stretches across the Four Corners area of southeastern Utah, southwestern Colorado, northeastern Arizona, and northwestern New Mexico. Over this vast area of unparalleled geologic scenery there are a multitude of national parks, monuments, and recreation areas; state parks; wilderness study areas; and primitive areas, which showcase the colorful canyons and weird erosional features.

A continuity of sedimentary formations underlies the Canyonlands region. Comprising mudstones, siltstones, sandstones, and conglomerates, these formations greatly influence the type and composition of plants that grow in the region. Often the soil type is an erosional residue of the parent formation, which may be just a few inches below the surface. The soils, climate, elevation, and rates of evaporation together create the rigorous growing conditions that limit plant growth and species composition in the region. However, there is a large number of common plants found throughout the Canyonlands region, and these plants are the focus of this book.

Not every plant in this book is found throughout the entire region; some species have a very narrow distribution while others grow across the Southwest. However, the plants of this field guide do represent a core of vegetation that one might see across the Canyonlands region. These plants are not restricted by political or park boundaries; they show an allegiance only to the colors of sandstone and shale.

Life Zones and Plant Communities

In the 1890s, the biologist C. Hart Merriam studied the vegetation and wildlife around the San Francisco Peaks near Flagstaff, Arizona, noting that there, as elsewhere in the West, were fairly distinct belts of vegetation across an elevational scale from the lowlands to the high alpine peaks. He distinguished and named these belts based upon their dominant vegetation. Merriam also found relationships between certain plants and animals in these belts, or "life zones," as he called them. From lowest to highest elevation, his six life zones are: Lower Sonoran, Upper Sonoran, Transition, Canadian, Hudsonian, and Arctic-Alpine. Although his life zones showed variation and tended to blend into one another, they have been a good way to broadly define the major ecological zones of the West.

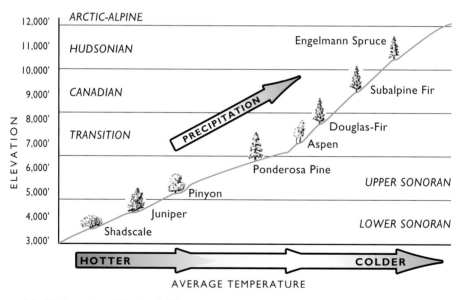

Modified version of Merriam's life zones

Since Merriam's time, ecologists have proposed different schemes to better define the plant communities on the Colorado Plateau. Each scheme offers a varying degree of precision; however, for its general purposes, this guidebook identifies the wildflowers, shrubs, and a few trees between the lower elevational grassland/shrubland (3,800–5,000') up through the pinyon-juniper woodland (4,500–7,000'). This constitutes the upper portions of what Merriam would classify as the Lower Sonoran Zone and the Upper Sonoran Zone, and also the lower limits of the Transition Zone.

Within this elevational span one can distinguish separate smaller divisions, or *microhabitats,* of plant communities and thus better illustrate some of the distributional ranges or habitat relationships of the plants. Characterized by the dominant woody and herbaceous plants, but also by alkalinity, moisture, and growing substrate, these simplified communities within our 3,800–7,000' elevational range are:

1. Salt Desert Shrub (StDS). Characterized by Shadscale, Greasewood, and Mormon Tea. Only plant species that can tolerate highly alkaline and saline soils occupy these geologic strata.

2. Lowland Riparian (RIP). Characterized by Fremont's Cottonwood, Water Birch, Boxelder, Willow, Tamarisk, Coyote Bush, Rabbitbrush, and Greasewood. The riparian zones are the verdant belts of vegetation along the canyon bottoms, riverbanks, and streambeds. Like an oasis in the desert, this ecological community attracts many species of birds and animals.

3. Hanging Garden (HG). Characterized by Maidenhair Ferns, Scarlet Monkeyflower, Helleborine, and Alcove Columbine. As water moves downward through the porous sandstone, it may encounter an impervious rock layer. At this point the water flows horizontally until it reaches an exposed edge of the sandstone or drips from an alcove wall. Hanging gardens are the lush plant communities in these alcoves; the highest number of endemic plants occurs within this plant community. These communities may also be present beneath the large pour-offs in the canyon drainages, regardless of rock type.

4. Blackbrush (Blk). Communities dominated by extensive stands of blackbrush across uniformly thin soils.

5. Sand Desert Shrub (SDS). Characterized by Old Man Sage, Yucca, Indian Ricegrass, and Shinnery Oak. Many of the plants in this community have extensive root systems that stabilize the sand dunes; others can "readjust" to shifting sands.

6. Mixed Desert Shrub (MDS). Can include a mixture of Rabbitbrush, Four-Wing Saltbush, Blackbrush, Narrowleaf Mahogany, and other species. Often different soil types overlap and intergrade in this community.

7. Cool Desert Shrub (CDS). Characterized by Big Sagebrush, Winterfat, and Rabbitbrush. This community is based on loamy or sandy soils.

8. Pinyon-Juniper Woodland (PJ). Characterized by Pinyon Pine, Utah Juniper, Singleleaf Ash, and Utah Serviceberry. This community covers a vast portion of Utah and the Canyonlands region. Plants occur on rocky soils or jointed bedrock.

9. Warm Desert Shrub (WDS). Characterized by Blackbrush and Old Man Sage, based on hot, dry slopes and rocky outcrops.

10. Ponderosa Pine (PP). Characterized by Ponderosa Pine and Aspen. Found in areas with drier soil types.

Another term used in this guide is **WEEDY,** which describes those plants that occur in disturbed or damaged sites nearly everywhere throughout the region. Many of these plants are not native to the Canyonlands region.

Soils and Other Environmental Conditions

There are two main aspects of soils—texture and chemical composition— that have direct effects upon plant growth and species composition. Unless sediments are carried by wind and water a long distance away, the weathering and erosion of a local sedimentary rock generally creates the various soil types found in an area. Erosion of the coarse-textured Navajo or Wingate sandstones results in sandy soils, while erosion of the shales and mudstones of the Mancos Shale or Morrison formations results in fine-textured soils. Each soil's moisture-holding capacity, which is important for plant survival, decreases from deep sandy soils, through rocky loams, to shallow fine-textured clays and silts. Since plants vary in their ability to survive in dry soils, some plants are present only in particular soil types.

Generally, coarse-textured soils are dominated by woody shrubs or trees with long taproots that can penetrate deep into the soil to reach water during periods of drought. Fine-textured soils, high in clays and silts, support grasses, low-growing perennials, and annual plants whose shallow-growing root systems can absorb available moisture in the surface and near-surface soil layers, especially right after a rain. Soils of intermediate texture support a mix of these two contrasting forms.

The soil's chemical composition, which is related to its texture, also influences the species of plants that grow in a location. For instance, soils high in sodium and alkalinity, such as those derived from the Mancos Shale Formation, inhibit plant growth and thus affect species composition. In this way, some species of plants are narrowly restricted to certain geologic strata and the soil conditions created by the erosion of that strata. One example is the Canyonlands Biscuitroot, *Lomatium latilobum,* which occurs along rock fins of the Entrada and Navajo sandstones in a few locations within the region.

Other environmental factors that affect plant distribution and species composition are elevation and aspect. With increases in elevation, temperature decreases and precipitation increases. Along this temperature/moisture gradient, the lowland plant communities, including semidesert grasslands and shrublands, give way to the pinyon-juniper woodlands and then to other forests at higher elevations. But elevation may be compensated for by aspect: north-facing slopes are generally cooler than south-facing slopes. Cool, moist alcove sites may contain plants usually found in the higher elevations, such as Douglas-fir trees (*Pseudotsuga menziesii*).

Annual precipitation, rates of evaporation, maximum summer temperatures, and the vegetation present are some other factors that define landscapes. Due to these characters, the Canyonlands region is a "cold desert"—a semiarid region, with a tendency towards cold winters and hot, dry summers. The average high and low temperatures are: 41°/21°F for the winter and 90°/60°F for the summer.

This elevational range receives an average of 9 inches of precipitation annually. Seasonal precipitation characteristically includes gentle, steady rains in winter and spring and brief but deluging cloudbursts in late summer. Snowfall varies considerably year to year, with the greatest average amounts falling in January, April, and November. It is not uncommon in April to have snow one week and 60°F temperatures the next.

Table 1. Climate information from Canyonlands National Park

	J	F	M	A	M	J	J	A	S	O	N	D
Temperature (in °F)												
Extreme High	67	75	85	91	101	109	111	108	108	94	80	68
Extreme Low	28	-21	7	16	23	32	38	36	28	-6	-8	-15
Average High	39	46	55	64	73	87	92	90	82	68	51	38
Average Low	19	23	30	34	46	58	62	60	51	40	29	22
Precipitation												
Rain (in inches)	.63	.29	1.07	.76	.71	.50	1.15	.92	.69	1.0	.86	.60
Snow (in inches)	5.5	1.2	2.8	3.4	0.2	–	–	–	–	0.5	3.3	2.4
Thunderstorms	0	1	1	4	4	9	11	5	2	0	0	0

Environmental Considerations

Endemic Plants

Primarily due to the unique geologic history and climate of the Colorado Plateau, there is a high level of plant endemism—plants restricted to a geographic region, topographical unit, or soil condition—in the Canyonlands region. Roughly 55 percent of the endemic plants on the Colorado Plateau occur on sand and gravel soils, and about 25 percent occur on clays, shales, or muds. Because of their limited distribution, a few are federally listed endangered or threatened species protected under the Endangered Species Act.

Cryptobiotic Crust

Cryptobiotic crusts are found throughout the world, but they are especially important on the Colorado Plateau. These crusts are dark brown to black, lumpy, and highly contoured, looking much like a cityscape in miniature. When young or poorly developed, they may be nearly invisible to the naked eye. Cryptobiotic crusts are important soil stabilizers in this sandy environment and aid plants in obtaining moisture and nutrients, especially nitrogen, from the soil.

Mosses, soil fungi, lichens, and green algae occur in these soils, but it is the cyanobacteria that make up the bulk of the crust and can make up 95 percent of the crust's biomass. The microscopic cyanobacteria secrete a thick, extracellular, gelatinous sheath that surrounds and coats their cells and the filaments they form. Soil particles adhere to this sticky sheath, making larger, more complex clumps that provide cohesion and strength to the soil. When moistened, filaments of the cyanobacteria partially extrude from the main sheath. These filaments produce new sheaths around themselves and leave the abandoned sheath material behind; there is more abandoned than inhabited sheath material in a well-developed crust.

Cryptobiotic crusts are very fragile and often protect the entire thin topsoil layer. Crushing the crusts severely inhibits their normal functions and may result in removal of the material and the topsoil via erosion. Rates of recovery vary depending upon the severity of the impact, precipitation, source material, and other factors, but some disturbed crusts may take over fifty years to recover.

When hiking in the desert avoid these soil crusts by staying on established trails or walking in sandy washes or on slickrock areas. Backtrack if necessary or look for game trails to follow to keep from crushing the soil crusts.

Plant Adaptations and Characteristics

Plants in the Canyonlands

There are many environmental conditions that plants must contend with in this desert environment: hot, dry summers; cold winters; strong, drying winds; long periods between rainfall; herbivory; intense solar radiation; and other rigorous growing conditions. Plants, unlike wildlife, are literally rooted in place and cannot relocate when drought or herbivores threaten. Plants have nevertheless adapted various physical or metabolic characteristics that enable them to live and thrive here.

In the Canyonlands region, total plant cover is not 100 percent, so plants rarely compete with each other for available light the way plants might in other environments. Instead, a plant's success depends more upon temperature, water, and available nutrients. During winter most plants are dormant or have greatly reduced growth rates; precipitation in winter and early spring recharges the soil moisture content. Springtime, before temperatures become too high or soil moisture too low, presents the optimal window for maximum photosynthetic rates for many plants.

The leaf is the main site where photosynthesis takes place. Water vapor, oxygen, and carbon dioxide move from within the leaf into the air, and vice versa, through lens-shaped openings called stomata. Located mainly on the underside of the leaf, away from direct sunlight, the stomata open and close with the demands of photosynthesis, while minimizing water loss to the desert air. Available sunlight for photosynthesis is not a problem for desert plants; losing excessive amounts of water during photosynthesis can be a problem.

To reduce this potential problem, desert plants share many physical and metabolic traits that help to conserve moisture. Small leaf size; various hairs or projections on the surface to reduce the drying effect of the wind; thick, waxy leaf surfaces; deep taproots or barely subsurface extensive lateral root systems; succulent stems (cacti); and evergreen or deciduous leaves are just a few ways plants have adapted to the desert environment.

Both leaf strategies, evergreen and deciduous, benefit desert plants. Evergreen leaves remain on the plant thoughout the year and are shed gradually so that the plant is never barren. This low energy expenditure for leaf production allows the plant to use that energy elsewhere. Deciduous plants lose their leaves at the end of the growing season as the plant enters a dormant period over the winter. By dropping the leaves, the plant does not need to expend energy on leaf maintenance during the non-growing months.

Not all plants put on their maximum growth in the spring, however. Certain species, like Rabbitbrush (*Chrysothamnus* sp.), have deep taproots and can continue photosynthetic activity throughout the summer drought period. Other species, like Cliffrose (*Purshia mexicana*), correlate plant growth and flowering with the onset of summer rains and can enter a second growth and flower phase in years with heavy August and September rainfall.

A combination of physical and metabolic characters help plants that grow in salty or saline soils. The weathering of certain formations, particularly the Mancos Shale and Chinle formations, results in high concentrations of salts in the upper levels of the soils, often in the root zone. Only certain plants can tolerate these highly alkaline soils that ordinarily would inhibit the growth of most plants. Salt-tolerant plants have evolved different ways of surviving in a saline environment. Winterfat (*Ceratoides lanata*) blocks the uptake of excessive salts at the roots. Saltbush (*Atriplex canescens*) has specialized structures on the leaf surface into which excessive salts are placed; these structures eventually rupture, excreting the salts to the outside. Other plants may deposit salts back to the soil via an internal return system. Adaptations to the desert environment have resulted in a variety of fascinating forms and interesting lifestyles, enabling plants to exist in this seemingly harsh landscape.

Energy from the Sun

Photosynthesis is the metabolic process by which plants use carbon dioxide from the atmosphere, solar energy, and chlorophyll to produce organic molecules—carbohydrates—necessary for plant growth. Another way of describing photosynthesis is that it is the conversion of light energy to chemical energy. Carbohydrates and simple sugars then are turned into more complex substances by enzyme activity. There are three pathways of photosynthesis, each distinguished by the first chemical reaction that happens upon the capture of carbon dioxide. All plants use one of these methods, and the efficiency of each varies with different temperatures and the amount of water available. Cacti use the CAM (Crassulacean Acid Metabolism) pathway, which allows the plant to open its stomata (portholelike openings) at night to capture carbon dioxide and store it in a cell chamber for use in the daylight. The plant completes the process of photosynthesis in the daylight. By opening the stomata at night, when temperatures are cooler, the plant reduces the amount of water it loses to the atmosphere.

THE FUNCTIONING PLANT

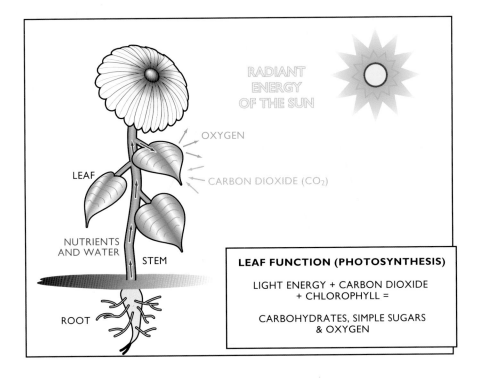

LEAF FUNCTION (PHOTOSYNTHESIS)

LIGHT ENERGY + CARBON DIOXIDE + CHLOROPHYLL =

CARBOHYDRATES, SIMPLE SUGARS & OXYGEN

The diagram above shows the general functions of a plant. Roots absorb water and minerals from the soil so they can be transported to the higher parts of the plant. The stem has conduits for transporting water and minerals to the leaves and for taking products made in the leaves—carbohydrates, proteins, lipids, etc.—to other parts of the plants. Leaves contain chlorophyll and other pigments necessary for photosynthesis. The sugars and other products of photosynthesis and the raw materials taken from the soil are either used immediately or stored by the plant.

Pollination

Flowers contain the structures necessary to complete pollination. *Pollination* is the transfer of male spores, or *pollen,* from the *anther* at the end of the *stamen* to the *stigma,* which is the tip of the female part of the flower, the *pistil.* When pollen grains reach the stigma they germinate, much like a seed, and a *pollen tube(s)* grows downwards into the *style,* the stalk of the pistil. In these tubes the male sex cells or *gametes* form. For most of the flowering plants (the angiosperms) in this book, the pollen tube grows through the tissues of the pistil. (The only gymnosperms in this book are Pinyon, Utah Juniper, and Mormon Tea.) The pistil nourishes the tube as it grows, and when the pollen tube is near the female gamete in the *ovule,* the male gametes release and fertilization takes place. The transfer of pollen to the stigma of a flower is one of the greatest technical achievements of the plant kingdom; the logistics of this have helped create the fascinating variety of flowers we see today.

The fossil record is a stone testament to the innovation of the plant kingdom over millions of years; it reveals spore-producing ferns, primitive fernlike trees that bore seeds (not spores), the cone-bearing plants (the conifers), and the more modern orchids with their specialized methods of pollination. Throughout this history there was a noted change from wind pollination to animal pollination, a conclusion we draw based upon the structure of fossilized flowers, which occurred at about the same time pollinating insects became numerous.

Generally there are three main ways ovules become fertilized: wind pollination, animal pollination (including insects, birds, and mammals), and self-pollination, which occurs in only a small percentage of plants. Wind pollination is considered the more "primitive" form of pollination; the gymnosperms and about 15 percent of the angiosperms, such as grasses and many trees, are wind pollinated. Wind pollination is a chancy method, and used primarily by plants that grow in close proximity to one another or where there are few insects to do the job. To increase the odds of pollination, many wind-pollinated plants release tremendous amounts of pollen into the wind from their usually smaller and less-showy flowers. Some have separate male and female flowers, often arranged in dense clusters, to further this strategy. Some species release their huge amounts of pollen before their leaves develop, in order to increase the odds of contact even more.

The evolution of animal pollination, which benefits both pollinator and plant, created a tremendous amount of variation in flower structure, since no single floral type can perfectly suit all types of potential pollinators. About 85 percent of all flowering plants are insect pollinated. Differences in flower size, shape, coloration, and arrangement are shown in the simplified chart of Table 2. This does not cover all the groups of insects, and one may observe many different types of insects on one flower.

Most insects move pollen from flower to flower more reliably than the wind. Some insects are generalists and visit different types of plants, not selecting just one type of flower during their foraging. Bees, on the other hand, are more "faithful" as pollinators—they select one or a few species of plants and regularly visit only those flowers, which count on the bees for pollination and reward them with nectar and pollen.

Plants tend to consistently attract certain insect pollinators, and those pollinators evolve to select the flowers that fulfill their needs as well. Nectar, a sugary bribe or reward, attracts the pollinators. Certain plants may time their nectar release to coincide with the times of peak foraging activity of certain insects or birds, thus do not spend precious energy providing nectar to non-pollinating species. For example, members of the penstemon (*Penstemon*) and Indian paintbrush (*Castilleja*) genera produce nectar twice a day, to coincide with the feeding periods of their pollinators. Nectar production at midday is conservative for members of the *Castilleja* genus that are hummingbird pollinated, due to the lowered activity period for the birds around midday.

One classic example of a pollination relationship is between the *Pronuba* or yucca moth (family Megathymidae) and the yucca (*yucca* sp.) plant. After mating, the female moth collects some sticky pollen grains and pollinates a flower. At the same time, she deposits her eggs in the flower's ovary. The developing larvae feed on some of the forming seeds as they mature, thus this tightly connected insect-plant relationship benefits both partners.

Visual acuity for insects is less than that for humans, and their ability to distinguish shape and form from a distance is relatively poor. Many flowers have developed special patterns of color, called *nectar guides*, which function as landing lights, attracting these pollinators and orienting them to the nectar. Most yellow and white flowers are highly reflective of light and are thus visited by a large variety of insects, but blue flowers are frequented more by bees than by any other insect group.

Table 2. Simplified chart showing some relationships between flowers and pollinator groups. (Adapted from Howe and Westley 1988)

Pollinator	Flower Color	Flower Depth	Odor
Beetles	Usually dull	Flat, bowl-shaped	Strong
Flies	Variable	Moderately deep	Variable
Bees	Blue, white, pink, but not pure red	Flat or broad tube	Usually sweet
Wasps	Dull or brown	Flat or broad tube	Usually sweet
Hawkmoths	White or pale green	Deep, narrow, tubular	Strong, sweet
Small moths	White or green (nocturnal); red, purple, pink (diurnal)	Moderately deep	Moderately sweet
Butterflies	Bright red, yellow, blue	Deep, narrow, tubular	Moderately strong, sweet
Birds	Bright red	Deep, with wide spur or tubular	None

Several plants also change their floral color after pollination. The flowers of Dwarf Evening-Primrose (*Oenothera caespitosa*) fade to a pinkish color; likewise, the central spot on several of the lupines (*Lupinus* sp.) fade from white to yellowish. Such color changes indicate that pollination has taken place, and tell insects to search for other flowers to pollinate.

Plant Characteristics

This section will help to define some of the terms and physical characteristics of the plants in this book. Technical terms are kept to a minimum; for their definitions see the **Glossary.**

Many desert plants are **perennials,** plants with more or less woody stems and deep or long roots that last at least three years. Two types of perennials exist: **woody** shrubs and trees, or **herbaceous** perennials that die back to underground roots or stems each winter. **Biennials** have a two-year life cycle. The plant becomes established during the first season, often producing a basal rosette of leaves. During the second season, the plant flowers, produces seed, and then dies. **Annuals** complete their life cycle in one growing season, their future housed in dormant seeds. Annuals require specific amounts of winter and spring moisture before the seed germinates; chemical inhibitors within the seed prevent premature germination. In drought conditions, the seeds do not germinate and remain dormant, possibly for many years.

Sometimes it is difficult to distinguish perennials from annuals. To identify perennials, look for woody stems; underground structures for food storage such as tubers, bulbs, and corms; or dried flowering stems and leaves from previous years.

Leaf Structure

Important features to note about the leaves and stems are:
- Arrangement of the leaves along the stem: are they opposite, alternate, or whorled?
- Simple versus compound leaves. If compound, how many leaflets?
- Leaf margin: entire, toothed, wavy, or lobed?
- Are the leaves only basal or are they also found along the stem?
- Does the leaf have a stalk (petiole)?
- Are there hairs or other projections along the stem or on the leaf surfaces?

Flower Structure

The diagram in Figure 2 shows a generalized flower in cross section. The variation and number of flower parts are key characters for identification. The **sepals,** or outer series of parts, surround the base of the flower. Sepals are often green and inconspicuous, but they may be colorful and showy as in the paintbrushes (*Castilleja*). Together they are called the **calyx,** which may be composed of separate or fused sepals.

Inside the calyx of most flowers are the **petals,** an inner series of generally colorful parts. Petals also vary in size and shape and may be separate or fused.

Figure 1. Variations of leaf arrangement (A), shape (B), and margin (C)

A. Leaf Arrangement

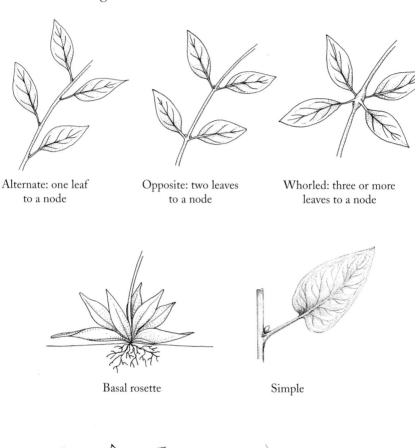

Alternate: one leaf
to a node

Opposite: two leaves
to a node

Whorled: three or more
leaves to a node

Basal rosette

Simple

Pinnately compound leaves: leaflets
arranged on both sides of the petiole

Palmately compound leaves: leaflets
spreading like fingers from the
palm of the hand

B. Leaf Shape

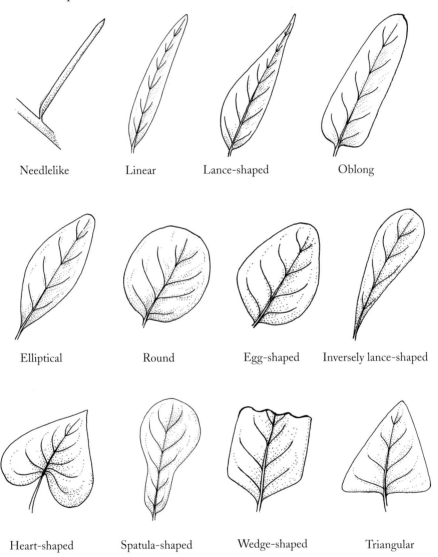

Needlelike

Linear

Lance-shaped

Oblong

Elliptical

Round

Egg-shaped

Inversely lance-shaped

Heart-shaped

Spatula-shaped

Wedge-shaped

Triangular

C. Leaf Margin

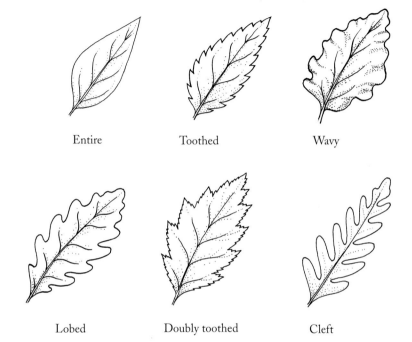

Entire   Toothed   Wavy

Lobed   Doubly toothed   Cleft

The petals are collectively called the **corolla**; some plants, however, may lack a corolla, or the sepals and petals may be identical. Together, the calyx and corolla function to attract pollinators and protect the sex organs at the center of the flower.

Inside the flower are the **stamens,** the pollen-producing structures. Typically long and thin, the stamens have a clublike or elongate appendage at the tip—the **anther**—from which pollen is released. Stamens may number from none to more than one hundred per flower.

The **pistil,** or seed-producing structure, has three main parts: stigma, style, and ovary. Pollen reaches the **stigma** or pollen receptor, which sits atop the stalklike **style.** The style connects the **ovary** and the stigma, and is the tubelike structure that the pollen tube grows through to reach the ovary. Within the ovary are the **ovules,** the structures that become the seeds after fertilization.

Here again, variation is the theme song. For example, some flowers lack a style; ovules may vary in arrangement and number, which determines the type of seed or fruit that develops. Many flowers have both male (staminate) and female (pistillate) parts within one flower, but some plants have separate male and female flowers on the same plant or even on separate plants. The term **monoecious** ("one home") is used to describe a species where male and female flowers are on one plant; **dioecious** ("two homes") refers to unisexual flowers being found on separate individual plants.

Two families with unique flower types are shown in Figures 3 and 4. These flowers are in the Sunflower (Asteraceae) and Pea (Fabaceae) families.

Members of the Sunflower Family (Asteraceae) have an elaborate flower arrangement. A **flower head**, which looks like one flower, is actually a dense cluster of a few to several hundred tiny flowers. The flower head has a series of **bracts**, more or less modified leaves, that surround the base of the flower head. The calyx of each of the tiny flowers is absent or reduced to bristles, scales, or hairs—the **pappus**—that form a crown of various character at the top of the seed; this is often a key in identifying the species. Members of the Asteraceae produce two types of flowers, **ray flowers** and **disk flowers**, and they may possess either one type of these flowers or both. See Figure 3 for generalized flowers of this family. A straplike limb forms the corolla of the ray flower and is usually brightly colored. The disk flower has a small, tubular corolla, usually with five lobes, but with no rays.

Members of the Pea Family (Fabaceae) have a calyx that surrounds five modified petals. The upper petal, or **standard**, is erect, spreading, and usually the longest of the five. The two side petals, or **wings,** closely surround the **keel,** which are the two fused lower petals. See Figure 4 for a typical flower of the Fabaceae.

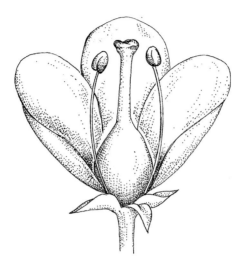

Figure 2. Typical flower in cross section

Classifying and Naming Plants

   Carl Linnaeus (1707-1778) was a Swedish naturalist who developed the modern system of binomial nomenclature, in which every living thing has a genus and species name. Linnaeus created a descriptive system that standardized the terminology and naming of plants and animals, as well as how to systematically organize the information. The system provides a common language for all to use. For instance, the binomial name *Mimulus eastwoodiae* (Scarlet Monkeyflower) consists of a Latin or Greek generic (referring to genus) name followed by a specific epithet (referring to species). Linnaeus based his work upon that done by various individuals all the way back to Aristotle; his work *Species Plantarum* (1753), for plants, and the tenth edition of his *Systema Naturae* (1758), for animals, form the foundations for scientific naming still in use today.

Figure 3. Flowers of the Sunflower Family (Asteraceae)

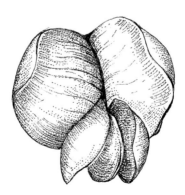

Figure 4. Flower of the Pea Family (Fabaceae)

For plants, he based his system, known as the sexual system, upon the number, union, or length of stamens and the structure of the ovary. Because such features do not necessarily show evolutionary relatedness, this has been called an artificial system. His system greatly clarified and simplified the identification and description of known and newly discovered taxa.

With Linnaeus's nomenclatural hierarchy, plants with similar sexual features were lumped together in families, then sorted out into different genera—finer divisions of the family group. The genera were then split into the various species. From the family level upwards to the level of kingdom, the groupings all have distinct endings. For all the family names, such as Asteraceae or Liliaceae, the ending is -aceae. Many of the scientific names provide clues as to features of the plant and/or its native range; its discoverer may also honor someone by giving the plant that person's name.

A Utah Flora by Stanley L. Welsh, N. Duane Atwood, Sherel Goodrich, and Larry C. Higgins is the primary botanical key for plants in Utah. All of the scientific names (except for a few family names) used in this field guide are from that text. Common names, which may vary, also follow those used in *A Utah Flora,* with a few exceptions, to provide additional consistency.

Using This Guide

This field guide covers 189 species of plants found in the Canyonlands region. Plants are separated into groups based upon flower color and then arranged alphabetically by family (Agavaceae, Apiaceae, etc.) and then by genus and species within the family. Scientific names are standardized, whereas common names are not, so the plants are not arranged alphabetically by common names.

To identify a flower, turn to the corresponding color section and search among those pages for the plant. Several plants are bicolored or may exhibit a range of colors because of genetic variation. If the plant does not appear within the primary color section, turn to the secondary color section and search there. Please note that a few of the photos in the book show fruits instead of flowers. This is because for some species, the fruits better define the plant or are visible longer during the growing season than the flowers.

Each plant has a brief **Description** section to provide identifying information, including characteristics such as the size, shape, form, and color of stems, leaves, flowers, and fruits. A hand lens is helpful in viewing minute structures such as hairs, bracts, flower parts, or seeds. See the illustrations in the plant characteristics section and the definitions in the glossary to help with descriptive terminology.

Vegetative Communities, listed after the final description sentence, are abbreviated as shown on page 29.

Flowering periods, shown in italics at the end of description information, are general ranges; these will vary with seasonal weather and elevation. The seasons are described below.

> Winter: *February-March 20*
> Early spring: *March 21-April 20*
> Spring: *March 21-June 20*
> Midspring: *April-May*
> Late spring: *June*
> Early summer: *June 22-July 21*
> Summer: *June 21-September 20*
> Midsummer: *July-August*
> Late summer: *September*
> Early autumn: *September 21-October 21*
> Autumn: *September 21-December 21*
> Midautumn: *October-November*

The **Comments** sections provide natural history information about the plant and often explain the derivation of the scientific name. If a plant is endemic to the Canyonlands region or is threatened or endangered, it is noted here. The comments sections also describe notable uses of a plant including medicinal properties or edibility. Those interested in historical or modern herbalism, homeopathy, or flower essences should check the reference section in the back of the book.

Some comparisons to similar species are noted; however, to include each of the more than one thousand species of plants found in the area would result in a much larger guide. If at times you are only able to determine the genus or family level of a plant, take heart; occasionally, even trained botanists are stumped.

Vegetative Communities Abbreviations

StDS	Salt Desert Shrub
RIP	Lowland Riparian
HG	Hanging Garden
Blk	Blackbrush
SDS	Sand Desert Shrub
MDS	Mixed Desert Shrub
CDS	Cool Desert Shrub
PJ	Pinyon-Juniper
WDS	Warm Desert Shrub
PP	Ponderosa Pine
WEEDY	Disturbed or Damaged Sites

WHITE FLOWERS

This section includes white, cream, and gray flowers, and those that grade into whitish shades of pink or blue.

DIANE ALLEN

Datil Yucca

DATIL YUCCA
Yucca baccata
Agave Family (Agavaceae)

Description: A dense basal cluster of stout, straplike leaves that are 12–40" long and 1–2" wide. Short stems are single or clumped together. Fibers along the leaf margins curl. Flowering stalks may barely rise above the leaves; bell-shaped flowers are 1¹/₂–3¹/₄" long and white to cream in color. Fruits large and fleshy at maturity. PJ.

Late spring–early summer.

Comments: The Ancestral Puebloans made cordage, mats, sandals, baskets, and cloth from the leaf fibers; they ate the flowering stalks, flowers, and fruits; and soap was made from the roots. *Baccata* (fruited) refers to the large pods.

HARRIMAN'S YUCCA
Yucca harrimaniae
Agave Family (Agavaceae)

Description: Solitary or clumped plant. Rigid leaves lance-shaped, pale green, sharp-pointed at the tip, and 4–20" long. With age, the white fibers curl along the leaf margins. Flower stalk rises above the leaves 14–30" or more. Greenish yellow to cream-colored flowers are bell-shaped, 1¹/₂–2" long, and tinged with purple. Capsule cylindrical with a short beak. WDS, CDS, PJ.

Midspring–early summer.

Comments: Native Americans plaited the tough plant fibers together to make cordage. Flower buds, flowers, and tender flower stalks are edible. Narrowleaf Yucca (*Y. angustissima*) is similar but has flatter, linear leaves, a white or pale green style, and longer flowering stems and flower clusters.

Harriman's Yucca

POISON IVY
Toxicodendron rydbergii
Cashew Family (Anacardiaceae)

Description: Woody shrub to 3', or sparsely branched single stems in a loose cluster. Compound leaves long-petioled with 3 (rarely 4 or 5) toothed or lobed, dark lusterless green, 1–4$^1/_2$"-long leaflets. Tiny, whitish male and female flowers are densely arranged in leaf axils on separate plants. Cream to yellow berries may remain over winter. RIP, HG.

Spring.

Comments: *Toxicodendron* (toxic plant) refers to the non-volatile oil, urushoil, on the leaves and stems, which may cause uncomfortable skin irritation. *Rydbergii* is for the botanist Per Axel Rydberg (1860-1931).

Poison Ivy

Tomentose Amsonia

TOMENTOSE AMSONIA
Amsonia tomentosa
Dogbane Family (Apocynaceae)

Description: Perennial, 8–24" tall, forming dense clusters of leaves and flowering stems. Leaves alternate, smooth, or densely hairy; lower ones lance-shaped and larger than the upper threadlike leaves. Bluish white flowers, borne in terminal clusters, have slender tube-shaped corollas, $^3/_8$–$^3/_4$" long, that flare at the top. Several-seeded pods contain brownish, cylindrical seeds. StDS, Blk, MDS.

Spring.

Comments: *Amsonia* is for Dr. Charles Amson, an eighteenth-century Virginia physician. *Tomentosa* refers to the wool-like covering created by the many small, matted, intermingled hairs.

Dogbane

WHORLED MILKWEED
Asclepias subverticillata
Milkweed Family (Asclepiadaceae)

Description: Plant to 4' high, with slender, usually unbranched stems. Threadlike leaves, up to 3" long, arise in opposite pairs or whorls of 3–5 leaves. Small-stalked flower clusters, with up to 20 flowers per cluster, found in the upper portion of the plant. Each white, star-shaped flower is less than $1/2$" long, with 5 white petals and 5 erect, white hoods. Slim seedpods rise upwards and are 2–4" long. CDS, MDS, StDS, PJ.

Late spring–midsummer.

Comments: Between the hoods on each flower are slits that can trap the leg(s) of a visiting insect. As the insect pulls its leg free, "saddlebag" structures of pollen attach to the leg. The insect then carries these to the next flower, which is thus cross-pollinated by the previous one. Whorled Milkweed is very poisonous.

DOGBANE
Apocynum cannabinum
Dogbane Family (Apocynaceae)

Description: Thin reddish stems with milky latex arise in spindly clusters to 3'. Stems and leaves branch oppositely or in a whorled pattern. Variably sized leaves are lance- or egg-shaped in outline, smooth above and downy beneath, and the lower leaves may be stemless. White flowers, $1/8$" wide, cup-shaped, and borne in clusters at the top or along short side-stems. Long, thin pods hang down at maturity. RIP.

Late spring–summer.

Comments: Also called "Indian hemp"; *cannabinum* (like hemp) refers to the strong cordage that was made by plaiting together the stem's long fibers. Cymarin, a chemical found in the roots, was used as a cardiac medicine, and was listed until 1952 in the *United States Pharmacopoeia*.

Whorled Milkweed

EMORY SEEPWILLOW
Baccharis emoryi
Sunflower Family (Asteraceae)

Description: Shrub 3–12' tall, many-branched; branches often striped. Leaves $^3/_8$–$3^1/_2$" long, linear or spatula-shaped, and irregularly toothed or entire along the margins. Female and male flowers in loose conical or pyramid-like clusters at the upper ends of the stems and on separate plants. Female flowers with several series of sticky bracts; seeds have fine, $^1/_2$"-long, white hairs. RIP, HG.

Late spring–early autumn.

Comments: *Baccharis* is in honor of the Greek god of wine, Bacchus, due to the sweet aroma of the root. *Emoryi* is for William H. Emory (1811–1887), an American soldier and lieutenant of topographical engineers in 1838. Called "seepwillow" because of its willowlike leaves and habit of growing in wet places.

Emory Seepwillow

STEVIA DUSTY-MAIDEN
Chaenactis stevioides
Sunflower Family (Asteraceae)

Description: Annual, $1^1/_2$–14" tall, very hairy throughout. Leaves up to 4" long, linear, grayish-woolly, and lobed or cleft usually halfway to the middle of the leaf; individual lobes may be smaller. One-inch-wide flower heads, solitary or clustered, arise on short stems. Stamens often protrude above the white disk flowers; some outer flowers may be enlarged and raylike. StDS, CDS, PJ.

Spring.

Comments: *Chaenactis* is from the Greek *chaino* (to gape) and *actis* (ray), referring to the enlarged, irregular, raylike outer disk flowers of many species.

Stevia Dusty-Maiden

JUDIE CHROBAK-COX

Rose-Heath

ROSE-HEATH
Chaetopappa ericoides
Sunflower Family (Asteraceae)

Description: Perennial, up to 6" tall, and may grow in loose clusters. Stems have small, stiff hairs. Leaves up to $^3/_8$" long, linear or spatula-shaped, and taper to a point. Flower heads are solitary or in clusters; the bracts that subtend the flowers are in 3–5 series. Each whitish flower has 12–25 rays, about $^1/_4$" long, surrounding a circle of yellow disk flowers. Seeds with hairs lying close to the surface. StDS, MDS, PJ.

Late spring–summer.

Comments: *Ericoides* (heathlike) refers to the overall small size and leaf pattern of the plant.

GRAY THISTLE
Cirsium undulatum
Sunflower Family (Asteraceae)

Description: Perennial, stems covered with dense white hairs, and 2–5' tall. Leaves form a basal rosette; leaves 2–10" long, deeply divided or lobed, and the lobes toothed or lobed with spines along the margin. Leaves along the stem smaller. Flower heads rounded, $1^1/_2$–$2^1/_2$" wide, creamy white or pink, and contain only disk flowers. Bracts below the heads brown, lance-shaped, and with the spiny tips spreading. MDS, CDS, PJ.

Midspring–early summer.

Comments: *Cirsium* is from the Greek name *kirsion* (swollen vein) because one species of thistle was used to treat swollen veins. *C. neomexicana*, the Utah Thistle, is similar but the flower heads are more cylindrical and the involucre is greenish and long-spined.

Gray Thistle

HORSEWEED
Conyza canadensis
Sunflower Family (Asteraceae)

Description: Annual, up to 40" tall, with smooth or slightly hairy stems that branch in the upper portion. Leaves ³/₄–3¹/₈" long, linear to inversely lance-shaped, and the margins with fine hairs. Flower heads numerous, urn-shaped, ¹/₈–¹/₄" tall, and the minute ray flowers white or purplish and surrounding about 20 yellow disk flowers. WEEDY, RIP.

Midspring–summer.

Comments: *Conyza* is the Greek name for the plant and *canadensis* (of Canada) refers to the plant's distribution.

Horseweed

Spreading Daisy

SPREADING DAISY
Erigeron divergens
Sunflower Family (Asteraceae)

Description: Annual, biennial, or short-lived perennial, 2–20" tall. Stems have soft, spreading hairs. Basal leaves inversely lance- or spatula-shaped, ³/₈–2¹/₂" long, narrow, and covered with hairs. Leaves along the stem similar but smaller. Flower heads may be numerous per plant, with 75–150 blue, pink, or white rays, about 1" wide, surrounding the yellow disk flowers. RIP, CDS, PJ.

Midspring–summer.

Comments: *Erigeron* is from Greek *eri* (early) and *geron* (old man), because the plants flower early in the season and the seed's bristles resemble an old man's gray hair.

JOEL S. TUHY

Vernal Daisy

VERNAL DAISY
Erigeron pumilis
Sunflower Family (Asteraceae)

Description: Perennial to 20" tall; lower branches clothed with ashy to brown withered leaves. Basal leaves linear or inversely lance-shaped, ¼–3½" long, and covered with coarse, stiff hairs. Stem leaves smaller or absent. Flower heads few to numerous, ¼–½" wide, and with 50–100 white or pink rays surrounding a cluster of yellow disk flowers. Bracts below the flower heads may have long, soft hairs. StDS, CDS, PJ.

Midspring–early summer.

Comments: *Pumilis* (dwarf) refers to the small stature of this hairy plant.

SILVERY TOWNSENDIA
Townsendia incana
Sunflower Family (Asteraceae)

Description: Short-lived perennial, ¾–4" tall; stems conspicuously covered with white hairs. Spatula- to inversely lance-shaped leaves are ¼–1½" long and hairy. Flower heads on short stalks are solitary or few, ½–1" wide, and with 13–34 rays that are white on the upper surface and pink to lavender below. StDS, MDS, CDS, PJ.

Midspring–early summer.

Comments: Named for David Townsend (1787–1858), an amateur botanist from West Chester, Pennsylvania.

Silvery Townsendia

CISCO WOODYASTER
Xylorhia venusta
Sunflower Family (Asteraceae)

Description: Perennial from a woody base; stems 4–16" tall and smooth or hairy. Inversely lance- or spatula-shaped leaves ³/₄–3¹/₂" long. Flower heads on stems 2–8" long. Heads ³/₄–5" wide; the bracts below the heads pointed. Ray flowers, 12–36, whitish to bluish or purplish, surround a cluster of yellow disk flowers. StDS.

Spring.

Comments: A Colorado Plateau endemic. Some years this woodyaster carpets the desert.

Cisco Woodyaster

YELLOW-EYE CRYPTANTH
Cryptantha flavoculata
Borage Family (Boraginaceae)

Description: Low-growing perennial, 4–16" tall, with 1 to several slender, hairy stems. Leaves linear to spatula-shaped, 1–4" long, and covered with short, stiff hairs. Corolla a short white tube with spreading lobes and a yellow throat. The four nutlets have rough surfaces. CDS, PJ.

Midspring–late spring.

Comments: Many members of the *Cryptantha* genus are identified by the minute variations on the seed's surface as well as by other features.

Yellow-Eye Cryptanth

Slender Cryptanth

SLENDER CRYPTANTH
Cryptantha tenuis
Borage Family (Boraginaceae)

Description: Low-growing perennial, 4–9" tall, with 1 to several stems arising from a basal cluster of leaves. Stem and leaves with stiff, short hairs. Leaves linear to spatula-shaped, mostly basal, and ³/₄–2³/₄" long. Flowers ³/₈–³/₄" long, the white corolla tube flaring to funnel-shaped at the tip and just longer than the calyx. StDS, Blk, MDS, CDS, PJ.

Midspring.

Comments: A Colorado Plateau endemic. A related plant, the Long-Flowered Cryptanth (*C. longiflora*), has flowers that extend far beyond the calyx tip.

WOODY TIQUILIA
Tiquilia latior
Borage Family (Boraginaceae)

Description: Perennial, forming dense mats 8–24" in diameter. Leaves linear or elliptical, ³/₈" long, with stiff hairs along the margins. Flowers funnel-shaped, ¹/₈" wide, whitish pink, and borne amongst the leaves. The 4 fruits are 1-seeded, clumped nutlets. StDS, CDS, PJ.

Spring–early summer.

Comments: The flowers of this Colorado Plateau endemic open in the afternoon.

Woody Tiquilia

RAVEN TENNYSON

Spectacle-Pod

SPECTACLE-POD
Dithyrea wislizenii
Mustard Family (Brassicaceae)

Description: Annual, with several to many erect stems to 20" tall. Basal leaves gray, wavy-toothed or irregularly lobed, 1–3" long, and covered with minute hairs. Leaves along the flowering stalk are smaller. Flowers white to greenish, $^3/_8$–$^3/_4$" wide, arising in ladderlike fashion; top flowers in a rounded cluster. Rounded seedpods, $^1/_2$" long, are fused together along a common midline. SDS.

Spring.

Comments: *Dithyrea* (two shields) describes the seedpods, which resemble a pair of eyeglasses. Named for Friedrich Adolph Wislizenus (1810–1889), a German physician, traveler, and author, who immigrated to the U.S. in 1835, joined a trading caravan to Mexico in 1846, and made many observations of the local flora and fauna.

WEDGELEAF
Draba cuneifolia
Mustard Family (Brassicaceae)

Description: Annual, 5" tall, with a basal rosette of wedge-shaped leaves covered with stiff hairs. Flowers white, $1/4$" long, arising on short stalks congested at the top of the main flowering stalk. The 4 whitish petals are spatula-shaped. Seedpods are flat, more or less elliptical, and contain 20 or more tiny seeds. WDS, MDS, PJ.

Mid–late spring.

Comments: *Draba* is the Greek name for a related plant, and *cuneifolia* (wedge-shaped leaf) describes the leaves.

Wedgeleaf

FREMONT'S PEPPERGRASS
Lepidium fremontii
Mustard Family (Brassicaceae)

Description: Bushy perennial, $1–2^3/4$' high. Mostly stem leaves, $1/2–3^1/2$" long and divided to the midrib with narrow lobes. Dense clusters of white, 4-petaled flowers, $1/4–1/2$" wide, borne at the ends of the stems. Small, rounded seedpods are slightly notched at the tip. Blk, WDS.

Spring–early summer.

Comments: *Lepidium* is from the Greek *lepis* (scale), a reference to the flattened shape of the edible, peppery seedpods. *Fremontii* is for John C. Frémont (1813–1890), an American explorer, soldier, and presidential candidate noted for his explorations of the West, including the Great Basin and the route to Oregon.

Fremont's Peppergrass

MOUNTAIN PEPPERPLANT
Lepidium montanum
Mustard Family (Brassicaceae)

Description: Perennial (or, less commonly, biennial), up to 4' tall. Leaves basal only or basal and along the stem, variously shaped, and $^1/_4$–5" long. Basal leaves may be cleft to the midline or entire; stem leaves narrow and entire along the margin. White flowers, 4-petaled, up to $^1/_8$" across and arranged in tight clusters. Seedpods $^1/_8$" long, wide, and egg-shaped. StDS, MDS, CDS.

Late spring–summer.

Comments: Seedpods are edible and peppery. The form of the plant is highly variable.

Mountain Pepperplant

LITTLE TWISTFLOWER
Streptanthella longirostris
Mustard Family (Brassicaceae)

Description: Wiry annual up to 2' tall. Bluish green leaves lance-shaped or elliptical in outline and the leaf edges toothed and wavy or smooth. Flowering stalk has a few small leaves and the urn-shaped flowers are 2-toned; the greenish or purplish sepals contrast with the white or purplish-veined petals. Long, narrow, pointed seedpods hang downwards. WDS, MDS, PJ.

Spring.

Comments: *Streptanthella* is the diminutive of *Streptanthus*, from the Greek *streptos* (twisted) and *anthos* (flower), referring to the twisted petals of the flower. *Longirostris* (long beak) refers to the seedpod's pointed tip.

Little Twistflower

Heartleaf Twistflower

HEARTLEAF TWISTFLOWER
Streptanthus cordatus
Mustard Family (Brassicaceae)

Description: Perennial with smooth stems, 1–3' tall. Basal leaves are spatula-shaped with toothed margins; bluish green, and with heart-shaped bases that clasp the stem. Flowers have 4 purple sepals that pinch inwards at the top, almost obscuring the 4 purple to chestnut-colored petals. The flattened pods are 2–3" long and curve upwards. Blk, MDS, PJ.

Early–midspring.

Comments: *Streptanthus* is Greek for "twisted flower," and *cordatus* "heartlike" refers to the heart-shaped base of the upper stem leaves.

ELEGANT THELYPODY
Thelypodiopsis elegans
Mustard Family (Brassicaceae)

Description: Biennial or short-lived perennial, with smooth stems (but may be densely hairy below), and 5–38" tall. Basal leaves ³/₈–2¹/₂" long, with margins entire or irregularly toothed; upper leaves smaller and linear to lance-shaped. Flowers small, 4-petaled, arising on short stems from a main flowering stalk, and pink to lavender or white with purplish veins. The narrow seedpods are 1¹/₂–2³/₄" long and curve upwards. CDS, MDS, PJ.

Spring.

Comments: *Elegans* (elegant) refers to the tall, graceful stature of the plant.

Elegant Thelypody

Tall Thelypody

TALL THELYPODY
Thelypodium integrifolium
Mustard Family (Brassicaceae)

Description: Biennial, with smooth stems, 2–10' tall. Basal leaves 2–12" long, lance- to spatula- or egg-shaped; the margins entire or toothed. Leaves along the stem are smaller, ³/₄–4" long, and elliptic or lance-shaped. Flowers arranged in a conical pattern, with each flower ¹/₄–³/₈" wide with white petals and purplish sepals. Pods are thin, ³/₈–1³/₄" long, and curved upwards. RIP, PJ.

Summer.

Comments: *Thelypodium* is from the Greek *thelys* (female) and *podoin* (foot), referring to the stalked ovary of many of the species in this genus. *Integrifolium* (entire leaves) refers to the lack of teeth or lobes along the leaf margins.

Fendler's Sandwort

FENDLER'S SANDWORT
Arenaria fendleri
Pink Family (Caryophyllaceae)

Description: Perennial and low-growing, forming cushions or mats, the clustered basal leaves are ¹/₈–2" long, straight, and pungent-smelling. Two to six pairs of leaves present along the flowering stem. Flowers in loose clusters, each ¹/₄–¹/₂" wide with 4 or 5 greenish sepals washed with purple and 4 or 5 creamy yellow to white petals. Fruit is a small capsule with 6 teeth. CDS, PJ.

Late spring–midsummer.

Comments: *Arenaria* is from the Latin *arena* (sand), a reference to the growing location of these plants. *Fendleri* is for Augustus Fendler, a German immigrant who collected many southwestern plants for Asa Gray, the famous Harvard botanist.

WINTERFAT
Ceratoides lanata
Goosefoot Family (Chenopodiaceae)

Description: Compact shrub, mostly 3' or taller; leaves and branchlets covered with dense long hairs. Linear or lance-shaped leaves $3/8$–$1^1/2$" long. Flower clusters borne in leaf axils towards the branch tips. Male and female flowers separate but on the same plant; male flowers 2–4 per axil and female flowers in dense clusters. Fruits covered with long white hairs. StDS, CDS, PJ.

Midspring–summer.

Comments: An important winter browse plant for wildlife and livestock. *Lanata* (wool-like) refers to the hairy branches, leaves, and fruits.

JUDIE CHROBAK-COX

Winterfat

GREENLEAF MANZANITA
Arctostaphylos patula
Heath Family (Ericaceae)

Description: Often a low-growing, sprawling shrub with gnarled stems and smooth, reddish brown bark. Leaves alternate, egg-shaped to elliptical, $3/4$–2" long, and yellow-green. The pink to white bell-shaped flowers are borne in loose, hanging clusters. Fruit is a white, green, or brown berry. PP, RIP.

Spring–early summer.

Comments: *Arctostaphylos* is from the Greek *arktos* (bear) and *staphule* (bunch of grapes), in reference to the clustered edible but tart fruit.

Greenleaf Manzanita

Fendler's Euphorb

FENDLER'S EUPHORB
Euphorbia fendleri
Spurge Family (Euphorbiaceae)

Description: Perennial, low-growing, with reddish purple stems, 2–8" long, and the sap a milky latex. Oval to lance-shaped leaves opposite and $^1/_4$–$^3/_8$" long. Tiny flower clusters resemble a single flower, but separate male and female flowers are arranged in these clusters. Below the flower cluster are two separate petal-like appendages. There are 15–35 male flowers to 1 female flower per cluster. Blk, StDS, MDS, PJ.

Spring–summer.

Comments: *Euphorbia* is in honor of Euphorbus, the Greek physician of King Juba of Numidia, a Roman province in North Africa. The milky sap of this plant can be applied to burns or insect bites for treatment, but most Euphorbs are toxic. Named *Fendleri* in honor of the botanist Augustus Fendler.

STINKING MILKVETCH
Astragalus praelongus
Pea Family (Fabaceae)

Description: Perennial, 4–36" tall, stems erect
and often forming clumps. Compound leaves
1–9" long, with 7–33 elliptical or lance- to
inversely lance-shaped leaflets. Leaflets slightly
hairy below. Flower stalks 1½–12" tall with
10–33 tightly clustered flowers. Greenish calyx
contrasts with the cream-colored corolla,
which is ½–1" long and often is tipped with
purple. Broadly elliptical seedpods are upright
or curve downwards. Blk, MDS, PJ.

Mid-late spring.

Comments: Fleshy seedpods become woody
with age and may remain attached to the withered stems over the winter. Grows in selenium-
bearing soils; plants may exude the unpleas-
ant odor of selenium, hence the common
name.

Stinking Milkvetch

Western Prairie-Clover

WESTERN PRAIRIE-CLOVER
Dalea oligophylla
Pea Family (Fabaceae)

Description: Perennial with smooth, clustered
stems, 16–36" tall. Compound leaves alternate,
½–2" long, with dark, dot-like glands, and
comprised of 4–9 elliptical leaflets that are
often folded in half. Tiny white flowers, with
4 narrow, petal-like segments fused with the
tube formed by the stalks of the 5 stamens;
flowers densely clustered at the tops of smooth
stalks. MDS, Blk, PJ, HG.

Midspring–summer.

Comments: Found in sandy drainages.
Crushed leaves are lemon-scented. Previously
called *Petalostemon,* in reference to the fused
stamens and petals.

Wild Licorice

WILD LICORICE
Glycyrrhiza lepidota
Pea Family (Fabaceae)

Description: Perennial, 1–4' tall. Compound leaves 3–6¹/₂" long, with 13–19 lance-shaped leaflets. Leaflets pointed at the tip, smooth above, and glandular dotted or slightly hairy below. Flowers arranged along an elongated axis with 20–50 flowers per axis. Calyx less than ³/₈" long, bell-shaped; corolla white to cream-colored and ³/₈–¹/₂" long. Pods ³/₈–³/₄" long and covered with hooked prickles. RIP, MDS, PJ.

Midspring–midsummer.

Comments: *Glycyrrhiza* is from the Greek *glykos* (sweet) and *rhiza* (root), referring to the sweet flavor of the roasted roots, which were eaten by Native Americans. *Lepidota* (scaly) refers to the brown scales on the leaves. European Licorice (*G. glabra*) is commercially used in cough syrups, laxatives, and confections.

COMMON HOREHOUND
Marrubium vulgare
Mint Family (Laminaceae)

Description: Perennial, 8–40" tall, with square-shaped stems densely covered with hairs. Leaves opposite, hairy, oval, with a rounded or pointed tip, deeply veined, and toothed along the margin. Dense cluster of tiny white flowers in leaf axils; corolla is 2-lipped; the upper lip erect and the lower lip spreading and 3-cleft. WEEDY.

Late spring–midsummer.

Comments: *Vulgare* (common) refers to the wide distribution of this Eurasian native, and hore is Old English for "hairy," referring to the leaves and stems. Used in syrups for coughs or lung ailments.

Common Horehound

FUNNEL LILY
Androstephium breviflorum
Lily Family (Liliaceae)

Description: Perennial, with a 1"-wide, buried bulb. Grasslike leaves may be curved or straight, with 1–3 per plant. Leafless flowering stalk bears small cluster of 3–8 dirty green or white ³/₄"-wide flowers with purple markings. Capsule is 3-lobed and ¹/₂" long. StDS, Blk, PJ.

Spring.

Comments: *Breviflorum* (short flowers) refers to the short flowers.

Funnel Lily

SEGO LILY
Calochortus nuttallii
Lily Family (Liliaceae)

Description: Perennial, from a bulb. Stems 3–18" tall with (usually) 3 long, linear, grasslike leaves. Several 1–1¹/₂"-wide flowers with 3 narrow sepals, which are greenish to purplish on the outside and pale on the inside, all borne together. Three large white, cream, or lavender petals have a pointed tip; a hairy gland is located in a patch of yellow on the inside base of the petal and is often bordered above by a purplish crescent. CDS, PJ.

Midspring–midsummer.

Comments: State flower of Utah; bulbs edible. *Calochortus* is from two Greek words meaning "beautiful grass," referring to the leaves. *Nuttallii* is for naturalist Thomas Nuttall (1786–1859).

JOEL S. TUHY

Sego Lily

JOEL S. TUHY

Alcove Death Camas

ALCOVE DEATH CAMAS
Zigadenus vaginatus
Lily Family (Liliaceae)

Description: Perennial, 1–3¹/₂' tall, in hanging gardens. Linear, straplike leaves are 8–27" long; lower leaves sheathed. Flowers borne on short stems along an elongated stalk that is 5–15" long. White sepals and petals, 3 each, are similar and difficult to distinguish from each other. Flowers ¹/₃–³/₄" wide; petals have a large gland at the base. HG.
Midsummer.

Comments: *Zigadenus vaginatus* grows in moist alcoves or hanging gardens, and the bulbs are poisonous; hence, the common name. *Zigadenus* (paired glands) and *vaginatus* (sheath) describe the flowers and leaves.

SAND VERBENA
Abronia fragrans
Four O'Clock Family (Nyctaginaceae)

Description: Perennial, with stems 7–32" tall, smooth or covered with glandular hairs. Leaves opposite, leaf blades lance- to egg-shaped or linear, ³/₈–3¹/₂" long, and covered with fine sticky hairs. White flowers are borne in dense clusters of 25–80 flowers. Flowers have a tube-shaped corolla, ³/₈–1" long, with lobed and wavy flare at the end. Blk, MDS, PJ, CDS, SDS.
Spring–early summer.

Comments: *Fragrans* (fragrant) refers to the sweet-smelling flowers that bloom at night. *Abronia* is from the Greek *abros* (delicate), referring to the flowers. Sand grains adhere to the sticky hairs on the leaves.

Sand Verbena

NARROWLEAF UMBRELLAWORT
Mirabilis linearis
Four O'Clock Family (Nyctaginaceae)

Description: Clump-forming perennial with upright, smooth stems 8–40" high. Leaves linear, ³/₄–4" long, and sparingly toothed. Generally 3 flowers arise from a group of fused bracts; flowers whitish or pink, ¹/₂" wide, the tube short and flaring, and the petal-like segments deeply lobed at the tip. Extended stamens unequal in length. StDS, CDS, RIP, HG, PJ.

Late spring–early autumn.

Comments: *Linearis* (linear) refers to the narrow leaves.

Narrowleaf Umbrellawort

Willow Gaura

WILLOW GAURA
Gaura parviflora
Evening Primrose Family (Onagraceae)

Description: Lanky annual or biennial, to 5' tall, the stems covered with glandular hairs. Elliptical to lance-shaped leaves are ³/₄–4" long; upper ones smaller. Numerous, delicate, whitish-pink flowers, ¹/₈–¹/₄" long, are borne along an elongated stem at the top of the plant. Fruits are rectangular, up to ³/₈" long, and contain 3–4 seeds. RIP.

Midspring–summer.

Comments: Grows in moist sites. *Gaura* is from *gauros* (proud), in reference to the erect flowers. The long, thin flower stalk may curl like a lizard's tail, hence another common name: "lizardtail."

Dwarf Evening-Primrose

DWARF EVENING-PRIMROSE
Oenothera caespitosa
Evening-Primrose Family (Onagraceae)

Description: Low-growing perennial, leaves forming a basal rosette. Leaves ¹/₂–8" long, long-stemmed, and the leaf blade toothed, lobed, entire, or deeply cleft to the midline. White flowers are 2–3¹/₂" wide; tube is 1–5" long, and the 4 petals are lobed. Yellow stamens and style extend far above the flower's throat. StDS, MDS, CDS, PJ.

Spring–midsummer.

Comments: *Oenothera* (wine-scented) refers to the use of the roots in winemaking. *Caespitosa* (low-growing) describes the stature of the plant. Flowers open in late afternoon and evening. Pollinated by nocturnal insects, the flowers turn pink after pollination.

PALE EVENING-PRIMROSE
Oenothera pallida
Evening-Primrose Family (Onagraceae)

Description: Perennial with reddish stems, 4–28" long, growing erect or low. Lance-shaped to elliptical leaves have various margins—toothed, lobed, entire, or deeply cleft—and are ³/₈–3¹/₂" long. Solitary white flowers, about 1¹/₂" wide, grow from the leaf axils. Flowers have 4 petals with yellow patches at the base. WDS, Blk, CDS, PJ.

Spring–late summer.

Comments: Flowers turn pink or lavender after pollination. *Pallida* (pale) refers to the petal color. Flowers open in the late afternoon or evening and last about 1 day.

Pale Evening-Primrose

SAN RAFAEL PRICKLY-POPPY
Argemone corymbosa
Poppy Family (Papaveraceae)

Description: Moderately branched perennial has stout, spiny stems and grows 8–36" tall. Leaves inversely lance-shaped, 1–6" long, armed with stout spines below (sparingly above), and lobed halfway to the middle of the leaf. White flowers $1^1/_2$–$2^1/_2$" wide with numerous yellow stamens, the outer petals as broad as they are long and the inner ones much broader than long. Capsule football-shaped and spiny. StDS, SDS.

Midspring–summer.

Comments: *Argemone* is from the Greek *argema* (cataract), a disorder of the eye that this plant was used to treat. Also used as a purgative in substitution for syrup of ipecac.

San Rafael Prickly-Poppy

Indian-Wheat

INDIAN-WHEAT
Plantago patagonica
Plantain Family (Plantaginaceae)

Description: Annual plants covered with dense woolly hairs. Leaves linear or narrow and inversely lance-shaped, pointed at the tip, and $^3/_8$–8" long. Flowering stalk leafless, may be shorter than the leaves; and the tiny flowers are densely packed together. Corollas are 4-parted. Blk, PJ, CDS, RIP, WEEDY.

Midspring–summer.

Comments: *Plantago* is from the Latin *planta* (sole of the foot), referring to the broad foot-shaped leaves of some species. *Patagonica* (of Patagonia) refers to the plant's distribution. Also called Woolly Plantain. Seeds have mucilaginous coat and make a laxative when soaked in water and then eaten.

ROSEATA GILIA
Gilia roseata
Phlox Family (Polemoniaceae)

Description: Compact perennials, may be shrublike with a woody base, and stems 2–15" long covered with soft, wavy hairs. Leaves mostly along the stems, deeply dissected with 2–4 pairs of lobes or entire, and $^1/_4$–$1^1/_2$" long. Numerous white flowers borne in dense, flat-topped clusters. Sepal lobes pointed and usually shorter than the $^3/_8$" corolla tube. White corolla tube flares to 5 points and extends beyond the calyx. Blk, PJ, StDS, CDS. *Midspring–midsummer.*

Comments: A Colorado Plateau endemic. Similar in appearance to Ballhead Gilia, *G. congesta,* whose flowers do not exceed the calyx and which seldom has a woody base.

JOEL S. TUHY

Roseata Gilia

WATSON'S SLENDERLOBE
Leptodactylon watsonii
Phlox Family (Polemoniaceae)

Description: Perennial, cushion-forming, mostly 4–20" wide. Leaves 3- to 9-cleft, spiny, and opposite. White flowers have 6 greenish, unequal sepals and usually 4–6 petals that form a short tube and flare to $^3/_8$–$^3/_4$" wide at the top. Blk, CDS, PJ. *Late spring–early summer.*

Comments: *Leptodactylon* is from the Greek *leptos* (thin) and *daktylos* (finger), referring to the narrow leaf segments.

Watson's Slenderlobe

JOEL S. TUHY

Desert Phlox

DESERT PHLOX
Phlox austromontana
Phlox Family (Polemoniaceae)

Description: Cushion- or matlike plant, mainly 2–12" wide, the stems covered with long soft hairs. Linear leaves opposite and ¹/₄–³/₄" long. White, blue, or lavender solitary flowers with a bell-shaped calyx; the corolla tube is ³/₈" long and flares to 5 lobes. Blk, MDS, PJ.

Spring.

Comments: *Phlox* is the Greek word for "flame," in reference to the brightly colored flowers of many species. *P. hoodii*, Carpet Phlox, is similar but with dense woolly hairs, spine-tipped leaves, and woolly hairs on the calyx.

Longleaf Phlox

LONGLEAF PHLOX
Phlox longifolia
Phlox Family (Polemoniaceae)

Description: Perennial, stems solitary but may be clumped. Mainly 1¹/₈–16" tall, plants are woody below; the linear to lance-shaped leaves are ³/₈–3" long. Flowers borne in loose clusters at the ends of the stems, with the central or terminal flower blooming first. Flowers ³/₈–³/₄" wide with a long corolla tube that is white, pink, or lavender. StDS, MDS, CDS, PJ.
Midspring–midautumn.

Comments: *Phlox* is the Greek word for "flame," referring to the brightly colored flowers of many species. *Longifolia* (long-leaved) refers to the long, narrow leaves, which also inspired the common name.

FREMONT'S BUCKWHEAT
Eriogonum corymbosum
Buckwheat Family (Polygonaceae)

Description: Clump-forming shrub, up to 4' tall and just as wide. Lance-shaped or elliptical leaves are ¹/₄–1¹/₂" long and smooth or densely covered with hairs on one or both sides. Flat-topped cluster of small, white flowers cloak the plant. Flowers lack petals; the petal-like sepals are ¹/₈–¹/₄" long. StDS, CDS, MDS, PJ.
Midsummer–autumn.

Comments: *Corymbosum* (corymblike) refers to the flat-topped arrangement of the flowers.

Fremont's Buckwheat

JOEL S. TUHY

Cushion Buckwheat

CUSHION BUCKWHEAT
Eriogonum ovalifolium
Buckwheat Family (Polygonaceae)

Description: Mound-forming perennial, 2–16" across. Basal leaves round or spatula-shaped and covered with woolly hairs. Leaf blades are $^3/_4$–$2^3/_8$" long and the petioles are up to 2" long. Leafless flowering stalks bear a rounded cluster of small white flowers striped with purple. The 6 petal-like segments are similar. StDS, MDS, PJ.

Early spring–early summer.

Comments: *Ovalifolium* means "oval leaves."

ALCOVE COLUMBINE
Aquilegia micrantha
Buttercup Family (Ranunculaceae)

Description: Perennial, 1–3' tall; stems may be covered with sticky hairs. Leaves mainly basal, 2 or 3 times divided, and the rounded lobes of the leaflets are cleft. Flowers are 1–3" long, white to cream-colored, and have 5 petals that end with long, tubular spurs. HG.

Midspring–late summer.

Comments: Found mainly in moist alcoves, this plant is endemic to the Colorado Plateau. *Aquilegia* (eagle) refers to the flower spurs, which resemble an eagle's talons.

Alcove Columbine

WHITE VIRGIN'S-BOWER
Clematis ligusticifolia
Buttercup Family (Ranunculaceae)

Description: Woody vine that may reach 30' or more in length. Compound leaves with 3–7 lance- or egg-shaped leaflets; the leaflets may be toothed along the edges. The small, inconspicuous flowers have white sepals but lack petals and may be few to many per flat-topped cluster. Seed heads like cotton balls; each seed bears a long, hairy tail. RIP.

Summer.

Comments: *Clematis* is the Greek name of a climbing plant, and *ligusticifolia* (with leaves like *Ligusticum*) refers to the leaves' resemblance to those of another plant.

White Virgin's-Bower

BIRCHLEAF BUCKTHORN
Rhamnus betulaefolia
Buckthorn Family (Rhamnaceae)

Description: Shrub, 3–8' tall, with alternate elliptical or egg-shaped leaves. Leaf petioles up to ³/₄" long; blades broad, 1–6" long, and with prominent veins. Flat-topped clusters of small white flowers grow in the angle between the leaf and the stem. Berrylike fruits are about ³/₈" long and red at maturity. HG.

Midspring–early summer.

Comments: Often found growing in rock crevices or hanging gardens. *Rhamnus* is the Greek name of the plant and *betulaefolia* (birchlike leaves) refers to the leaves' resemblance to those of the birch.

Birchleaf Buckthorn

Utah Serviceberry

UTAH SERVICEBERRY
Amelanchier utahensis
Rose Family (Rosaceae)

Description: Low to large shrub, 1¹/₂–13' tall, reddish stems intricately branched. Oval to egg-shaped or elliptical leaves are ³/₈–1¹/₈" long, finely toothed along the margin mainly near the tip, and mostly hairy on one or both sides. White or pinkish fragrant flowers, ³/₈–³/₄" wide, with gaps between the spatula-shaped petals. Berries are seedy and purplish to pinkish. RIP, PJ, CDS.

Late spring.

Comments: Native Americans and early settlers added the mealy fruits to dried meat and animal fat to make pemmican. Derivation of *Amelanchier* is obscure; *utahensis* (of Utah) alludes to the first recorded specimen, which was from Washington County, Utah.

Apache Plume

APACHE PLUME
Fallugia paradoxa
Rose Family (Rosaceae)

Description: Shrub with scaly bark, growing up to 6' tall. Wedge-shaped, alternate leaves are ¼–¾" long with 3–5 lobes and green and scaly above. White flowers, ½–1" across, have 5 sepals, 5 petals, and numerous stamens. Seeds have long, featherlike hairs. RIP, Blk, CDS, MDS, PJ.

Midspring.

Comments: Named for Fallugius, a late-seventeenth-century botanist and churchman. Wood has been used for arrow shafts and broom handles. The feathery seeds resemble the war headdress of the Apache Indian, hence the common name.

ROCKMAT
Petrophytum caespitosum
Rose Family (Rosaceae)

Description: Mat-forming shrub up to 3' or more wide. Spatula- or inversely lance-shaped leaves, ⅛–¾" long, have long, straight hairs on one or both sides or are smooth. Flowers arranged in a dense cluster at the end of a short stem; the tiny petals are white. HG.

Summer–early autumn.

Comments: Often found in hanging gardens, the plants either form a dense mat over the rock surface or hang freely from the wall attached only by the stout root, hence its name: *Petrophytum* (rock plant). *Caespitosum* (low-growing) refers to the matlike form.

Rockmat

CLIFFROSE
Purshia mexicana
Rose Family (Rosaceae)

Description: Many-branched shrub with shredded bark, mainly 1¹/₂–8' tall. Leaves ¹/₈–⁵/₈" long, mostly 5-lobed, and glandular dotted and resinous. Flowers white to cream or yellowish, with 5 petals, ¹/₂–1" wide, and with many stamens. Long-tailed hairs attached to the seeds. Blk, PJ, MDS.

Midspring–summer.

Comments: Plants may be cloaked with fragrant flowers. *Purshia* is for Frederick T. Pursh (1774–1820), author of one of the earliest floras of North America. *Mexicana* refers to the range of the plant: southwest to central Mexico. A refreshing tea may be made from the leaves.

Cliff-Rose

Bastard Toadflax

BASTARD TOADFLAX
Comandra umbellata
Sandalwood Family (Santalaceae)

Description: Semi-parasitic perennial, stems erect, and 3–13" tall. Linear, lance-shaped, or narrowly elliptical leaves are ³/₈–1¹/₄" long and smooth. Flowers lack petals; the 5 sepals are whitish green. Purplish or brown fleshy layer coats the 1-seeded fruit. Blk, MDS, RIP, HG, CDS, PJ.

Spring.

Comments: *Comandra* is from the Greek *kome* (hair) and *andros* (man); the stamens are hairy at their base. *Umbellata* (umbel-like) refers to the flat-topped flower clusters. Known to parasitize over 200 plant species, Bastard Toadflax is also an alternate host for hard pine rust disease.

Fendlerbush

FENDLERBUSH
Fendlera rupicola
Saxifrage Family (Saxifragaceae)

Description: Many-branched shrub, 3–6' tall; bark of the twigs is reddish, turning gray with age, and longitudinally ridged and grooved. Opposite leaves linear or elliptical, ³/₈–1¹/₈" long, with sparse soft hairs and a prominent midrib. White flowers solitary or 2–3 together at the ends of short branches. The 4 petals are narrow at the base and ³/₈–1¹/₈" long. Fruit is a woody capsule, often persistent on the plant. Blk, MDS, PJ.
Midspring–early summer.

Comments: *Fendlera* is for Augustus Wilhelm Fendler, botanical explorer and collector in the American Southwest. *Rupicola* (growing on rocks) describes the plant's habit of growing in rocky areas. Native Americans used the hard wood of the shrub for digging tools and arrow foreshafts.

ABAJO PENSTEMON
Penstemon lentus
Figwort Family (Scrophulariaceae)

Description: Perennial, 12–20" tall, with smooth stems. Basal leaves spatula-shaped, ³/₄–4" long; stem leaves broadly inversely lance-shaped and stemless. Flowers are borne in leaf axils in clusters, white (on the west side of the Abajo Mountains) or blue to violet (on the east side of the Abajos). The corolla is tube-shaped, ¹/₂–1" long, and the lobes spread flat at the opening. CDS, PJ.
Late spring–midsummer.

Comments: A Colorado Plateau endemic, the variety *albiflorus* is found on the west side of the Abajo Mountains and near Natural Bridges National Monument. *Albiflorus* (white flower) refers to the flower color and is another common name for the plant: Whiteflower Penstemon.

Abajo Penstemon

SACRED DATURA
Datura wrightii
Potato Family (Solanaceae)

Description: Annual or perennial, often in rounded clumps, 1–4½' tall, and covered with dense, fine, gray hairs. Leaves large, 2–10" long; the blades egg-shaped, toothed along the margin, and with short, white hairs. Green sepals have lance-shaped lobes. Whitish to violet trumpet-shaped corollas are 5–9" long and about as wide. The golfball-shaped fruit is covered with prickles. Blk, CDS, PJ.

Midspring–late summer.

Comments: A poisonous narcotic plant formerly used to induce visions. The large flowers open in the evening and are pollinated by a host of night-flying insects and moths.

Sacred Datura

Tamarisk

TAMARISK
Tamarix chinensis
Tamarisk Family (Tamaricaceae)

Description: Shrub to moderately sized tree, with reddish brown bark and intricate branching. Scalelike leaves minute and juniper-like. Fragrant, white to pinkish flowers borne in elongated clusters; flowers have 5 sepals and 5 petals. RIP.

Midspring–early summer.

Comments: Introduced from Eurasia for erosion control in the West, Tamarisk spread to Utah around 1880 and by the 1920s was established along the Colorado River and its tributaries. Tamarisk is named for the Tamaris River in Spain; *chinensis* (of China) refers to its Eurasian distribution.

YELLOW FLOWERS

*This section includes yellow, golden, and
yellowish orange flowers. Some flowers have
mixed colors, especially the members of the
Sunflower Family where the ray and disk
flowers are often different colors;
they are included in this section.*

SKUNKBUSH
Rhus aromatica
Cashew Family (Anacardiaceae)

Description: Compact, densely branched shrub mainly 2–8' tall. Branchlets brown and flexible, become gray with age. Leaves simple and lobed or separated into 3 leaflets; leaflets lobed and smooth or minutely hairy on one or both sides. Tiny yellowish flowers arranged in dense clusters along short branches appear before the leaves in early spring. Fruit is a hard, lentil-sized seed within a fleshy reddish orange covering. HG, RIP, MDS.

Early spring.

Comments: Regionally known as Squawbush. Native Americans still collect the supple, grayish branchlets for their basketry. The crushed leaves have a disagreeable odor; hence, the common name, Skunkbush. Fruits are high in vitamin C and a refreshing but sour drink can be made by soaking the seeds in water. Wildlife also eat the berries.

Skunkbush

Sweetroot Spring-Parsley

SWEETROOT SPRING-PARSLEY
Cymopterus newberryi
Carrot Family (Apiaceae)

Description: Plant $2^3/_4$–7" tall, but leaves spread laterally along the ground. Leaves trisected into three deeply lobed or divided leaflets; individual lobes or leaflets are again lobed or toothed. Small, sticky hairs on leaves and stems are often coated with sand grains. Clusters of small, yellowish flowers are arranged at the top of a leafless stem. Seeds are $^1/_4$" long with crinkled, corky margins. Blk, SDS, PJ.

Spring.

Comments: *Cymopterus* is Greek for "wavy wing," referring to the wavy margin along the winged fruits. The parsniplike taproot can be eaten raw or cooked. *Newberryi* honors the geologist John Strong Newberry (1822–1892).

Canyonlands Biscuitroot

CANYONLANDS BISCUITROOT

Lomatium latilobum
Carrot Family (Apiaceae)

Description: Plants often in dense clumps, 4–20" tall, growing from a branched woody base. Leaves divided into 3–4 pairs of lateral, dull green, elliptical leaflets that may be lobed or toothed. Flower stalks smooth and $1^1/2$–$10^1/2$" tall. Short stems bear flat-topped clusters of yellowish flowers that arise from a common point. Seeds flat and wide with lateral wings. PJ, MDS.

Mid–late spring.

Comments: A Colorado Plateau endemic, biscuitroot grows mostly in Arches National Park and Colorado National Monument, in association with Entrada Sandstone. Native Americans ate the roots raw or pulverized them into a flour; hence, the common name. *Lomatium* (fringed) refers to the winged fruit, and *latilobum* (broad lobes) refers to the shape of the leaf.

PARRY'S LOMATIUM
Lomatium parryi
Carrot Family (Apiaceae)

Description: Plant 3–16" tall, arising from a short, branched, woody base. Leaves are highly dissected, dark green, and with 7–9 opposite pairs of primary leaflets branching from a main leaf stem. Reddish when young, the leafless flower stalks are 2–24" tall, topped by a cluster of tiny yellow flowers that turn white with age. Seeds are $1/2$" long, flattened, and with lateral wings. Blk, PJ.

Early–midspring.

Comments: Flowers bloom before the leaves develop; the previous season's dried leaves may still be present when the plant blooms. Named for Charles Christopher Parry (1823–1890), an American botanist who was the first official botanist of the U.S.D.A. Parry made notable botanical surveys of the American West and discovered numerous plants.

Parry's Lomatium

LOUISIANA WORMWOOD
Artemisia ludoviciana
Sunflower Family (Asteraceae)

Description: Perennial herb to 3' tall, often growing in dense clusters. Stemless leaves narrow, up to 4" long, pointed at the tip, and densely covered with white hairs on the undersides. Leaves range from green to white on the upper surface and may be lobed or toothed along the edges. Numerous small, yellowish flower heads occur along an elongated stem. RIP, PJ.

Midsummer–autumn.

Comments: A fragrant plant, *Ludoviciana* means "of St. Louis"; the plant was first recorded there by Thomas Nuttall (1786–1859), a botanist and naturalist who traveled in the western frontier.

Louisiana Wormwood

Budsage

BUDSAGE
Artemisia spinescens
Sunflower Family (Asteraceae)

Description: Low shrub to about 1' tall. After blooming, when the flowers have fallen, the flowering stems become inch-long spines. Leaves ¼–¾" long, grayish hairy, and finely divided into 5–7 3-parted lobes. The flower heads are yellow, about ¼" high and wide, and made of 6–20 flowers or more. The outer disk flowers are fertile, the inner ones sterile. StDS, Blk, CDS, PJ.

Early–midspring.

Comments: Often grows in saline soils. Common name derived from the clusters of leaves and flowers, which resemble buds. *Spinescens* (spiny) refers to the inch-long spines. Budsage recovers quickly from overbrowsing.

BIG SAGEBRUSH
Artemisia tridentata
Sunflower Family (Asteraceae)

Description: Shrub, averaging 2–7' tall, with a stout trunk and shaggy bark. Leaves silver-gray, hairy, wedge-shaped, ¼–2" long, and 3- to 5-toothed at the tip. Nonlobed leaves may appear in the early winter. Flowering stems generally surpass the vegetative branches and contain numerous side branches that bear dense clusters of tiny flower heads. Flowers have a cream-colored corolla. Seeds are tiny, black, and smooth. CDS, PJ.

Summer–midautumn.

Comments: The most common sagebrush of the mesa and plains habitat in the Southwest, it is also the state flower of Nevada. *Tridentata* (3-toothed) refers to the plant's usually having 3 lobes on the leaves. Leaves are very fragrant.

Big Sagebrush

RUBBER RABBITBRUSH
Chrysothamnus nauseosus
Sunflower Family (Asteraceae)

Description: Low to tall shrub, 1–7' tall; bark obscured by a dense, woolly covering of hairs. Leaves linear and flat, up to 4" long, hairy or smooth, and narrow at the tip. Flower heads numerous and arranged in flat-topped clusters at the terminal ends of branches. Disk flowers are yellow to yellow-orange; the small seeds have numerous bristles. StDS, PJ, RIP.

Summer–autumn.

Comments: *Chrysothamnus* is from Greek *chrysos* (golden) and *thamos* (a shrub). *Nauseosus* means heavy-scented, and refers to the smell of the leaves and flowers. The flowers make a bright yellow dye; a latex, used in manufacturing rubber, also comes from the plant. There are many subspecies of *C. nauseosus*.

Rubber Rabbitbrush

Bush Encelia

BUSH ENCELIA
Encelia frutescens
Sunflower Family (Asteraceae)

Description: Bushy shrub, 1–4' tall, with erect stems. Leaves alternate and toothed or entire along the margins, egg-shaped to rounded or lance-shaped, and up to 1" long with stiff hairs that lie close against the surface. Showy flowers are $^3/_8$–$1^3/_8$" wide and solitary. Yellow ray flowers may be lacking or, on average, 1–16, or possibly more; $^3/_8$" long; and surrounding a dense cluster of yellow disk flowers. Blk, StDS.

Late spring–summer.

Comments: *Encelia* is in honor of Christopher Encel, a sixteenth-century botanist. *Frutescens* means "becoming shrubby." The resin that exudes from the stem of a related plant, Brittlebush (*E. farinosa*), was burned as an incense by Spanish priests in the Southwest, which gave rise to another common name, "incienso." Native Americans chewed the resin for pain relief.

Scale Glandweed

SCALE GLANDWEED
Dyssodia pentachaeta
Sunflower Family (Asteraceae)

Description: Low perennial, 3–12" tall, form-ing rounded clumps. Leaves opposite, divided into 3–5 rigid linear lobes, $^1/_4$–$^3/_4$" long, and with coarse, stiff hairs. Flower heads borne on a $^3/_8$–3" long stalk. Each head is shaped like a top, $^1/_4$–$^3/_8$" wide; involucre bracts with yellow, oily glands. Yellow ray flowers, usually 13; the 50–70 disk flowers are dull yellow. Blk, StDS.

Midspring–late autumn.

Comments: *Pentachaeta* (5 scales) refers to the 5 pappus scales. Leaves are ill-smelling. The oil glands are visible with a hand lens.

NAKEDSTEM
Enceliopsis nudicaulis
Sunflower Family (Asteraceae)

Description: Perennial, 4–24" tall, with leaf-less flowering stalks arising from a woody base. Stout stem has dense, white hairs. Broadly rounded to egg-shaped leaves have a long petiole and are covered with fine, silvery hairs around the base of the stem. Solitary, coarse flower heads are ³/₄" high and over 2" wide. Each head has 13–21 yellow rays that surround a dense cluster of yellow disk flowers. Blk, MDS, PJ.

Spring–midsummer.

Comments: *Enceliopsis* (similar to *Encelia*) refers to the resemblance to another genus in the Asteraceae. *Nudicaulis* (naked stem) refers to the leafless flowering stalk. The related *E. nutans*, Noddinghead, has flat, rounded leaves and a solitary flower head that is rayless.

Nakedstem

Hopi Blanketflower

HOPI BLANKETFLOWER
Gaillardia pinnatifida
Sunflower Family (Asteraceae)

Description: Perennial, stems 3¹/₈–22" tall and generally with leaves halfway up the stem. Hairy leaves, up to 3" long, are usually lobed or wavy; the lobes may reach halfway to the midrib of the blade. Solitary flower heads on long stems have 7–12 yellow rays that surround a dense cluster of brownish purple disk flowers. Rays often 3-lobed; the entire flower head has some long, soft hairs. Blk, StDS, PJ.

Midspring–early summer.

Comments: *Gaillardia* is after M. Gaillard de Charentoreau, an eighteenth-century French magistrate and patron of botany. *Pinnatifida* (pinnately lobed; cleft leaves) describes the leaves. The Hopis used the plant as a diuretic.

Broom Snakeweed

BROOM SNAKEWEED
Gutierrezia sarothrae
Sunflower Family (Asteraceae)

Description: Perennial, rounded shrub to 3' tall, the branches resembling a broom. Two types of leaves present: linear stem leaves $^3/_4$–$2^3/_4$" long, and smaller ones that grow in small clusters between the stem and the main leaves. Flower heads, up to $^1/_8$" wide, arranged in flat-topped clusters of 3–10 flower heads together. Three to seven yellow ray flowers surround 3–8 yellow disk flowers. WDS, SDS, CDS, PJ.

Summer–autumn.

Comments: *Sarothrae*, from the Greek *sarotan* (broom), refers to the broomlike appearance of the stems. *Gutierrezia* is for Pedro Gutierrez, a nineteenth-century botanist of Madrid. An indicator species of disturbed land, snakeweed is toxic to livestock.

ERECT GUMWEED
Grindelia fastigiata
Sunflower Family (Asteraceae)

Description: Perennial, with smooth stems, averaging 2–4' tall. Leaves $^1/_2$–$5^1/_8$" long, inversely lance- to broadly lance-shaped, the margins entire or toothed. Flower heads $^1/_2$" wide and primarily disk flowers but may have an outer row of small, yellow ray flowers. Bracts that subtend the flower heads are in 6 rows, with the bracts bent outwards on some rows. Bracts and flowers sticky to the touch. MDS, RIP.

Summer–early autumn.

Comments: *Grindelia* is for David Hieronymus Grindel (1776–1836) a professor at Riga, Latvia. *Fastigiata* refers to the upright, clustered branches. Gumweed is a source of grindelia, a spasmodic used medicinally to stimulate the mucous membranes in the treatment of chronic bronchitis and asthma. *G. squarrosa*, Curlycup Gumweed, is similar but has large ray flowers and strongly curled involucre bracts.

Erect Gumweed

PRAIRIE SUNFLOWER
Helianthus petiolaris
Sunflower Family (Asteraceae)

Description: Annual, 2–48" tall, stems smooth or covered with short, stiff hairs. Alternate leaves petioled, the blades up to $3^1/s$" long and lance-shaped to rounded in outline. Leaf margins entire or with some serrations and short, stiff hairs. Flower heads solitary or several per stalk, 2–4" wide, with yellow ray flowers surrounding a cluster of brownish purple disk flowers. StDS, MDS, PJ, RIP.

Midspring–summer.

Comments: *Helianthus* (sunflower) refers to the flower's habit of turning with the sun. Sunflower seeds are consumed by small rodents and birds.

Prairie Sunflower

Hairy Goldenaster

HAIRY GOLDENASTER
Heterotheca villosa
Sunflower Family (Asteraceae)

Description: Perennial with several to many stems, often forming sprawling clumps 7–20" tall. Inversely lance-shaped to elliptical leaves have moderately stiff hairs. Flower heads, $^1/_2$" wide, are few to numerous per flowering stalk, each head with 10–25 yellow rays, $^1/_4$–$^3/_8$" long, that surround a compact cluster of yellow disk flowers. Seeds tipped with white, hairy bristles. StDS, PJ, CDS, Blk, RIP.

Spring–midsummer.

Comments: A very common plant; *villosa* (soft-hairy) refers to the gray hairs on the leaves and stems. The yellow flower heads resemble an aster, hence the common name.

Hyalineherb

HYALINEHERB
Hymenopappus filifolius
Sunflower Family (Asteraceae)

Description: Perennial, with clustered smooth or woolly stems, growing 2–24" high or taller. Basal leaves finely dissected, grayish hairy, and 1¹/₈–8" long; the upper leaves smaller or lacking. Flower heads are solitary or in small clusters, conical to bell-shaped, with 10–59 yellow disk flowers per head. WDS, StDS, SDS, PJ.

Late spring–early summer.

Comments: *Hymenopappus* is from the Greek *hymen* (membrane) and *pappus* (down), referring to the membranous scales on the crown of the seed. *Filifolius* (threadlike leaves) refers to the fine divisions of the leaf blade.

STEMLESS WOOLLYBASE
Hymenoxys acaulis
Sunflower Family (Asteraceae)

Description: Perennial. Leaves basal, the mostly leafless flower stalk up to 2' tall and smooth or with soft hairs. Narrow basal leaves, ³/₈–2³/₈" long, sometimes end in a short, abrupt tip. Stem leaves, if present, are few and small. Flower heads solitary or in pairs; bracts that subtend the flower head are in 2–3 unequal series. Ray flowers, 5–9, lobed at the tip, surround a small cluster of yellow disk flowers. MDS, PJ.

Spring–early summer.

Comments: *Hymenoxys* is from the Greek *hymen* (membrane) and *oxys* (sharp), in reference to the pointed pappus scales. *Acaulis* (without a stem) refers to the very short woody base of the plant. Native Americans made a stimulating beverage from the leaves and also applied the leaves as a local anesthetic.

Stemless Woollybase

DESERT DANDELION
Malacothrix sonchoides
Sunflower Family (Asteraceae)

Description: Annual, 2–14" tall, the stems often branching from the base. Stems smooth or with short, yellowish, glandular hairs. Basal leaves up to 4½" long and 1" wide, deeply divided, and the lobes toothed. Flower heads solitary or few per cluster, about ½" across, and the ray flowers are 5-lobed; lacks disk flowers. Blk, MDS, CDS, PJ.

Late spring–early summer.

Comments: *Malacothrix* is from the Greek *malakos* (soft) and *thrix* (hair), referring to the soft hairs of the pappus.

Desert Dandelion

ROCK GOLDENROD
Petradoria pumila
Sunflower Family (Asteraceae)

Description: Perennial, with numerous clustered stems 3–12" long and the base covered with dark to ash-colored withered leaves. Leathery leaves, linear to elliptical to lance-shaped, 1–5" long, and clustered at the base of the stems; stem leaves smaller. Clusters of 2–8 yellow flower heads, ¼" wide, have 1–3 ray flowers and are arranged in a flat-topped pattern. MDS, PJ.

Summer–early autumn.

Comments: *Petradoria* (rock-growing) refers to the habit of growing on or near rock surfaces. *Pumila* (dwarf) refers to the short stature of the plant.

Rock Goldenrod

Nakedstem Bahia

NAKEDSTEM BAHIA
Platyschkuhria integrifolia
Sunflower Family (Asteraceae)

Description: Perennial, stems solitary or few; individual plants may be clustered. Stems $4^1/_2$–24" tall with white hairs. Main leaves near base petioled, the blades $^1/_2$–4" long, and egg- to lance-shaped. Flower heads 2–10 per stem, the 7–11 yellow ray flowers surrounding a cluster of yellow disk flowers. StDS, PJ.

Late spring–early summer.

Comments: The common name was inspired by the leafless flowering stem. Grows in clay soils.

GREENSTEM PAPERFLOWER
Psilostrophe sparsiflora
Sunflower Family (Asteraceae)

Description: Perennial, often forming round bushes; the stems $5^1/_2$–24" tall and moderately to densely hairy at the bases, less so upwards. Leaves $^1/_2$" long and narrow, linear, or spatula-shaped. Flower heads $^3/_8$–$^3/_4$" wide, usually with 3 5-lobed yellow ray flowers surrounding a few yellow disk flowers. StDS, PJ, CDS.

Late spring–early autumn.

Comments: The common name comes from the ray flowers, which become papery when mature. *Sparsiflora* (sparse-flowered) refers to the few small, scattered flowers.

Greenstem Paperflower

UINTA GROUNDSEL
Senecio multilobatus
Sunflower Family (Asteraceae)

Description: Perennial, with stems mainly 4–24" tall and several stems per plant. Basal leaves spatula- to egg-shaped and deeply dissected; the lobes irregularly toothed or rounded. Flower heads $^3/\mathrm{s}$–1" wide in flat-topped clusters and with 7–13 narrow yellow ray flowers that surround a dense cluster of yellowish disk flowers. White hairs on seeds. Blk, PJ.

Late spring–midsummer.

Comments: *Senecio* is from Latin *senex* (old man), referring to the fluffy white hairs on the seeds, which resemble an old man's beard. *Multilobatus* (many-lobed) describes the leaves.

Uinta Groundsel

BROOM GROUNDSEL
Senecio spartoides
Sunflower Family (Asteraceae)

Description: Perennial, 8–40" tall, stems stout and often in clumps. Leaves smooth, $^3/\mathrm{4}$–4" long, linear, mostly undivided, and along the entire stem. Flower heads few to many in flat-topped clusters; each head $^3/\mathrm{s}$–1" wide with 4–8 yellow ray flowers per head surrounding a small cluster of yellow disk flowers. Seeds with bright white hairs. PJ, CDS.

Midsummer–midautumn.

Comments: A colorful plant that blooms in the late summer.

Broom Groundsel

Goldenrod

GOLDENROD
Solidago canadensis
Sunflower Family (Asteraceae)

Description: Perennial, with stems 1–5' tall or more that are minutely downy in at least the upper half, smooth below. Stem leaves are narrow, possibly sharp-toothed along the margins, ³/₄–4" long, and show three distinct veins. Flower heads borne on one side of a curved stem. Individual heads small with 10–17 yellowish ray flowers surrounding a tiny cluster of yellowish disk flowers. RIP.

Late spring–early autumn.

Comments: *Solidago* (to make whole) refers to the healing properties of Goldenrod; a tea brewed from the leaves was used for intestinal disorders and to promote sweating in cases of fever. Flowers make a yellow dye.

SCAPOSE GREENTHREAD
Thelesperma subnudum
Sunflower Family (Asteraceae)

Description: Perennial, with stems 1–20" tall. Leaves mainly basal, opposite, ³/₄–3" long, divided to the midrib, with the lobes linear. Flower stalks leafless; heads ¹/₄–³/₄" wide. Small outer bracts below the heads lance-shaped and bent. There are often 8 yellow ray flowers (sometimes none), ³/₈–1¹/₈" long and lobed at the tip, surrounding the yellow disk flowers. MDS, StDS, PJ.

Midspring–midsummer.

Comments: Dried flowers and young leaves make an excellent tea, hence another common name, "Navajo tea." *Thelesperma* is from the Greek *thele* (nipple) and *sperma* (seed), in reference to the small pointed projections on the seeds.

JOEL S. TUHY

Scapose Greenthread

Yellow Salsify

YELLOW SALSIFY
Tragopogon dubius
Sunflower Family (Asteraceae)

Description: Biennial, with erect stems 1–3¹/₂'. Leaves grasslike, linear, 2–10" long, and may have loose tufts of woolly hairs. Flower stalk inflated below the flowering head; long-pointed bracts below the flowering head longer than the lemon-yellow ray flowers. Disk flowers yellow. Flower head becomes an airy, 3–4"-wide globe of long whitish hairs attached to the seeds. RIP.

Late spring–summer.

Comments: *Tragopogon* is from the Greek *tragos* (goat) and *pogon* (beard) because the flower head bracts resemble a goat's beard. Roots were soaked to remove the bitterness, then peeled and eaten raw or stewed; their flavor is similar to that of oysters, hence another common name: "oyster-plant."

Rough Mulesears

ROUGH MULESEARS
Wyethia scabra
Sunflower Family (Asteraceae)

Description: Perennial, often in dense, sprawling clumps 1–3' tall and as wide or wider. Stems and leaves covered with rough, stiff hairs. Leaves linear to elliptical, 1–7" long. Flower heads 1–3" wide and generally solitary at the terminal ends of the branches. Yellow elliptical rays, 10–23, surround a dense cluster of yellow disk flowers. Blk, MDS, PJ.

Late spring–early summer.

Comments: Named for Nathaniel Wyeth (1802–1856), a Massachusetts businessman who led 2 overland expeditions to Oregon in 1832 and 1834. The botanist Thomas Nuttall and the ornithologist John Kirk Townsend accompanied the second expedition, during which Nuttall named this plant for Wyeth. *Scabra* (rough) refers to the texture of the leaves.

COCKLEBUR
Xanthium strumarium
Sunflower Family (Asteraceae)

Description: Annual with rough-hairy, mottled, purple stems, 7–40" or taller. Oval to egg-shaped or triangular leaves arise on long petioles and are ³/₄–5" long; leaf margins toothed with many lobes. Yellow flower heads few to many in small clusters that arise in the angle between the stem and the leaves. Seedpod ³/₈–1¹/₂" long and covered with stout, hooked prickles. RIP.

Summer–autumn.

Comments: *Xanthium* is the Greek name for the plant. *Strumarium* (rough) refers to either the texture of the stems or the burs. Seedlings are poisonous to livestock and may cause a skin rash on people.

Cocklebur

FREMONT'S MAHONIA
Mahonia fremontii
Barberry Family (Berberidaceae)

Description: Evergreen shrub, 4–5' or taller, with spreading branches. Compound leaves have 3–9 bluish green, 1"-long, smooth leaflets. Leaflets have 5–7 broad, triangular, spine-tipped teeth or lobes. Yellow flowers, $^1/_2$" wide, have 6 petals. Fruits are purplish or reddish seedy berries. WDS, MDS, StDS, PJ.

Early–midspring.

Comments: *Mahonia* is for Bernard M'Mahon (1755–1816), an Irish immigrant to the United States who ran a plant nursery in Philadelphia. Flowers are very fragrant and berries are edible. Pulverized roots make a yellow dye. *Fremontii* is for the explorer John C. Frémont.

Fremont's Mahonia

Yellow Cryptanth

YELLOW CRYPTANTH
Cryptantha flava
Borage Family (Boraginaceae)

Description: Perennial, 4–16" tall, often with clustered stems. Foliage, flower stems, and sepals densely covered with stiff hairs. Linear or inversely lance-shaped leaves are $^3/_4$–3" long and mainly basal. Dense clusters of yellow flowers, $^1/_4$" wide, have five petals that flare open at the top of a short tube. Small, arching crests encircle the open mouth of the tube. MDS, StDS, CDS, PJ.

Spring–early summer.

Comments: *Cryptantha* is from the Greek *krypto* (to hide) and *anthos* (flower), in reference to the bracts obscuring the flowers on some of the species. *Flava* (yellow) describes the flower color.

RAVEN TENNYSON

Showy Stoneseed

SHOWY STONESEED
Lithospermum incisum
Borage Family (Boraginaceae)

Description: Low-growing perennial, but may reach 20" tall. Dark green, linear leaves, up to 3" long, have small hairs pressed close to the surface. Trumpet-shaped yellow flowers, each with a long, thin corolla tube that flares into 5 ruffled lobes. Flowers are 1" wide and the toothed lobes have fine hairs. Fruit is a hard, white nutlet. CDS, PJ, MDS.

Spring.

Comments: *Lithospermum* (stone seed) refers to the hard nutlet. *Incisum* (toothed) refers to the lobes of the flowers. Stimulating teas were made from stems, leaves, and roots.

WALLFLOWER
Erysimum asperum
Mustard Family (Brassicaceae)

Description: Perennial or biennial, 6–30" tall. Basal leaves up to 4" long and linear, elliptical, or spatula-shaped. Leaf margins may be toothed, and the surface has fine Y-shaped hairs. Stem leaves linear, up to 4" long, with toothed margins. Flower stem bears dense clusters of yellow or yellowish orange flowers that are ³/₄" wide and have 4 petals. Seedpods up to 4" long. WDS, CDS, PJ.

Spring.

Comments: This species demonstrates the greatest ecological distribution of all Utah plants, growing from 2,490' to 12,467' in elevation.

Wallflower

DANDELION BLADDERPOD

Lesquerella rectipes
Mustard Family (Brassicaceae)

Description: Perennial with low-growing or erect stems up to 16" long that arise from a woody base. Base may have withered leaves. Basal leaves elliptical or inversely lance-shaped, up to 3" long, and smooth or toothed along the margins. The few leaves along the flowering stem are linear. Yellow flowers, with 4 petals, are about ½" wide. Fruits are rounded to elliptical inflated pods. Blk, WDS, PJ.

Spring–early summer.

Comments: Named after Leo Lesquereux, a late nineteenth-century American paleobotanist. This is the most common of the tall species of *Lesquerella* in southeastern Utah.

Dandelion Bladderpod

NEWBERRY'S TWINPOD

Physaria newberryi
Mustard Family (Brassicaceae)

Description: Low-growing, 1–9" tall, with withered leaves attached to the base. Basal leaves up to 3" long, with rounded blades egg- or spatula-shaped, with a small point at the tip. Leaves along the flower stalk smaller. Yellow flowers, each with a short flower stalk, are in tight clusters. Each flower has 4 spatula-shaped petals and is ¼–½" wide. Inflated seedpod has a deep indentation between the two halves. WDS, StDS, PJ.

Late winter–early summer.

Comments: *Physaria* is from the Greek *physa* (bladder), referring to the inflated seedpod. *Twinpod* comes from the seedpod's shape, which is like two balloons glued together. The species was named for John Strong Newberry (1822–1892), professor of geology at Columbia University.

Newberry's Twinpod

Tumbling Mustard

TUMBLING MUSTARD
Sisymbrium altissimum
Mustard Family (Brassicaceae)

Description: Annual, with stems 10–40" tall with coarse stiff hairs near the base but smooth above. Basal leaves lobed or highly divided and 3/8–8" long. Upper leaves linear and thread-like. Four-petaled yellow flowers, 1/8–1/4" wide, are borne on short stems. Long, narrow pod curves upwards. WEEDY.

Spring–early summer.

Comments: The wind uproots the mature, dry plant and blows it across the land, scattering seeds like a tumbleweed. Seeds and young plants edible.

PRINCE'S PLUME
Stanleya pinnata
Mustard Family (Brassicaceae)

Description: Perennial, branching near the base, stems up to 4' tall. Lower leaves deeply dissected, 1/2–6" long and 3/4–1 1/2" wide. Upper leaves narrowly lance-shaped or elliptical. Elongated flowering stalk bears clusters of lacy yellow flowers, 3/4–1 1/2" long, with the stamens protruding above the 4 petals. Seed-pods long-stalked, narrow, and up to 3" long. StDS, MDS, CDS, PJ.

Midspring–midsummer.

Comments: *Stanleya* is for Lord Edward Stanley (1755–1851), president of the Linnaean and Zoological societies in London. *Pinnata* (pinnate) refers to the deeply dissected leaves. Presence of this species indicates selenium-bearing soils.

Prince's Plume

JOEL S. TUHY

Common Pricklypear

COMMON PRICKLYPEAR
Opuntia erinacea
Cactus Family (Cactaceae)

Description: Plant 4–12" tall and up to 3' wide; the large, flattened pads spatula- or egg-shaped, smooth, and 2–8" long. Spines 4–9 per cluster, $1/4$–4" long, white, flattened at the base, and straight or curved slightly downward. Flowers $1^1/2$–$3^1/2$" wide and yellow, bronze, pink, or violet. Dry fruits are tan to brown and spiny. StDS, MDS, Blk, PJ, CDS.

Late spring–early summer.

Comments: *Opuntia* is a Greek name for a spiny plant that grew near Opus, Greece. Common Pricklypear may hybridize with several other species of *Opuntia*, making identification difficult. *O. polyacantha*, the Plains Pricklypear, is the other common *Opuntia* in the region.

Yellow Beeplant

YELLOW BEEPLANT
Cleome lutea
Caper Family (Capparidaceae)

Description: Annual, 1–5' tall with stout stems. Alternate leaves have 3–7 elliptical or lance-shaped leaflets, $3/8$–2" long, arising from a common point like fingers from the palm. Flowers have a short stalk, 4 petals, and 6 to many stamens that protrude above the top of the flower. Seed capsule, $3/8$–$1^1/2$" long, hangs downward on long stalk. WDS, MDS, SDS, PJ.

Spring–summer.

Comments: Flowers were boiled by Native Americans to make a black pigment for pottery paint. *C. serrulata*, Rocky Mountain Beeplant, has purplish flowers.

FOUR-WING SALTBUSH
Atriplex canescens
Goosefoot Family (Chenopodiaceae)

Description: Shrub, averaging $2^1/2$–3' tall. Leaves $3/8$–$1^1/2$" long, alternate, linear to inversely lance-shaped, and covered with small scales. Inconspicuous male and female flowers usually found on separate plants. Yellow male flowers grow in tiny globular clusters; female flowers grow in open clusters that are 2–16" long. Flattened seeds have 4 large membranous wings. Blk, StDS, CDS, PJ.

Midspring–midsummer.

Comments: *Atriplex* is the Latin name for the plant, and *canescens* (grayish white) refers to the color of the leaves. In the past, the ground seeds were cooked as cereal, the leaves were cooked and eaten, and the ashes of the plant were used as a leavening for breads. Some Pueblo groups still use the plant. Also a valuable browse plant for wildlife.

Four-Wing Saltbush

SHADSCALE
Atriplex confertifolia
Goosefoot Family (Chenopodiaceae)

Description: Spiny shrub, 1–3' tall, with in-conspicuous male and female flowers found on separate plants. Leaves alternate, blades ³/₈–³/₄" long, elliptical to oval, and covered with small scales on both sides. Yellow male flowers in small, tight clusters up to ³/₈" long. Female flowers generally in leaf axils near branch tips. Fruit is a tiny seed. StDS, CDS, PJ.

Spring–midsummer.

Comments: Grows in saline soils; the fish-scale-like leaves are edible but salty. *Confertifolia* (with flowers pressed together) refers to the tight floral clusters.

Shadscale

ROUNDLEAF BUFFALOBERRY
Shepherdia rotundifolia
Oleaster Family (Elaeagnaceae)

Description: Evergreen shrubs, 3–6' tall and 3–12' wide. Oval to egg- or lance-shaped leaves are ¹/₄–1¹/₂" long, silvery green above, and pale-hairy below. Yellowish flowers grow in the leaf axils and may be solitary or few to a cluster. Elliptical fruit has star-shaped hairs. Blk, PJ.

Midspring–early summer.

Comments: Endemic to the Colorado Plateau. *Rotundifolia* refers to the rounded leaves. Westward settlers used the cooked berries to make a sauce for buffalo steaks; hence the common name buffaloberry.

Roundleaf Buffaloberry

Yellow Milkvetch

YELLOW MILKVETCH
Astragalus flavus
Pea Family (Fabaceae)

Description: Perennial, with stems 2–12" tall, growing erect or curved upwards, and covered with star-shaped hairs. Compound leaves 1¹/₈–6" long, with 9–21 linear to egg-shaped leaflets that are ¹/₄–1" long. Leaves smooth or with short, stiff hairs. Flower stalk bears 6–30 flowers; calyx tube hairy and bell-shaped; the corolla ¹/₄–¹/₂" long and yellow. Seedpods erect and oblong, up to ¹/₂" long, and covered with short, stiff hairs. StDS.

Mid–late spring.

Comments: *Flavus* (yellow) refers to the flower color. Grows in fine-textured clay soils.

YELLOW SWEET-CLOVER
Melilotus officinalis
Pea Family (Fabaceae)

Description: Annual or biennial, with stems 2–5' or more and covered with stiff hairs pressed close to the surface. Compound leaves have short petioles; 3 leaflets wedge-shaped or elliptical, ¹/₄–1¹/₂" long, and with toothed margins. Flower stalk bears 20–65 yellow flowers that are about ¹/₄" long. Seedpods contain 1–2 seeds and are ¹/₈" long. WEEDY, RIP.

Midspring–summer.

Comments: Introduced from Europe; *Melilotus* (honey plant) refers to the plant's use in the honey industry. *Officinalis* means that it was officially sold as an herb or used in medicine; used in teas to treat intestinal worms or earaches or as a poultice for swollen joints.

Yellow Sweet-Clover

GOLDEN PEA
Thermopsis montana
Pea Family (Fabaceae)

Description: Stems 1–3' tall, clustered, and may have fine hairs. Leaves compound; 3 leaflets $3/4$–$3^1/2$" long, elliptical to lance-shaped, and pointed or rounded at the tip. Flower stalk with 2–23 pea-shaped yellow flowers, $3/4$–$1^1/8$" long. Slightly hairy pods turn black at maturity. PJ, RIP.

Late spring–early summer.

Comments: *Thermopsis* is from the Greek *thermos* (lupine) and *opsis* (resemblance), referring to the plant's likeness to the lupines. *Montana* (mountain) refers to the plant's higher-elevation distribution.

Golden Pea

GOLDEN CORYDALIS
Corydalis aurea
Fumitory Family (Fumariaceae)

Description: Annual or biennial, $2^1/2$–15" tall, and clump-forming. Leaves compound; linear to oblong leaflets several times divided. Flower stem bears few to many yellowish, $1/2$–$3/4$" long flowers with 4 petals. Outer pair of petals generally hooded above; 1 petal spur-shaped at the base. WDS, CDS, PJ.

Summer.

Comments: *Corydalis* is from the Greek *corydallis* (crested lark), in reference to the spur-shaped petal, which resembles the claw of a lark.

Golden Corydalis

JOEL S. TUHY

Desert Stickleaf

DESERT STICKLEAF

Mentzelia multiflora
Stickleaf Family (Loasaceae)

Description: Stout-stemmed perennial, 1–3'
tall. Upper portion of the stem and leaves have
rough, coarse hairs. Lower leaves lance-shaped,
$3/4–2^1/4$", with lobes halfway to the midrib; the
lobes rounded or toothed. Leaves are sticky;
sand often sticks to their surfaces. Upper leaves
smaller. Yellowish flowers borne in small clusters; flowers $1/2–3/4$" wide with the 5 outer
petals longer and wider than the inner ones.
Fruit an urn-shaped capsule. StDS, WDS,
CDS.

Late spring–midsummer.

Comments: Named for Christian Mentzel
(1622–1701), a German botanist. *Multiflora*
(many flowers) refers to the quantity of flowers, which open in the afternoon.

LAVENDER EVENING-
PRIMROSE

Calyophus lavandulifolia
Evening-Primrose Family (Onagraceae)

Description: Low perennial, $3/4–9$" tall.
Leaves $1/4–1^1/2$" long, linear to inversely lance-
shaped, covered with dense hairs, and with
wedge-shaped bases. Solitary yellow flowers
grow in the leaf axils; corolla tube is $3/4–3$" long
and the 4 flaring petals have ruffled edges. Blk,
StDS, MDS, PJ, CDS.

Late spring–midsummer.

Comments: The yellow flowers fade to shades
of orange or lavender upon drying, hence the
common name. *Lavandulifolia* (lavenderlike
leaves) refers to the resemblance of the leaves
to those of lavender.

Lavender Evening-Primrose

BRIDGES EVENING-PRIMROSE
Oenothera longissima
Evening-Primrose Family (Onagraceae)

Description: Biennial or perennial, with stems 3–6' or taller. Elliptical or lance- or inversely lance-shaped leaves 3/4–10" long with entire or wavy-toothed edges. Solitary yellow flowers, up to 4 1/2" long, with a long tube, borne in upper leaf axils. Upright capsules split at maturity and release numerous tiny black seeds. RIP.

Summer–midautumn.

Comments: A plant of moist sites. Type specimen is from Natural Bridges National Monument, hence the common name. *Longissima* refers to the long corolla tube. *O. elata,* Hooker's Evening-Primrose, is similar but with a shorter corolla tube.

Bridges Evening-Primrose

Winged Buckwheat

WINGED BUCKWHEAT
Eriogonum alatum
Buckwheat Family (Polygonaceae)

Description: Perennial, mainly 1–4' tall. Stout stem arises from a basal cluster of leaves, these often withered but still attached. Lance- or inversely lance-shaped leaves 1 1/8–5" long and covered with stiff, short hairs. Stem leaves smaller and fewer upwards. Flowers lack petals; petal-like sepals are yellowish to greenish and borne in clusters. Seeds are 1/4" long and have 3 wings. Blk, PJ.

Summer.

Comments: *Eriogonum* (woolly knee) refers to hairs located at the swollen stem joints of many species in this genus. *Alatum* (winged) refers to the seed's wings.

Desert Trumpet

DESERT TRUMPET
Eriogonum inflatum
Buckwheat Family (Polygonaceae)

Description: Annual or perennial, mostly 1–3' tall, with smooth, greenish or brownish, hollow stems that are inflated near the joint. Basal leaves long-stalked; blades rounded and up to 1¹/₈" wide with wavy margins. Many-branched flowering stalks arise from a common point; minute, yellowish or reddish, petal-less flowers are borne along slender branches. StDS, Blk, PJ.

Spring–midsummer.

Comments: *Inflatum* (inflated) refers to the shape of the stem. Native Americans ate the young stems raw or cooked.

BUR BUTTERCUP
Ranunculus testiculatus
Buttercup Family (Ranunculaceae)

Description: Annual, with hairy stems trailing along the ground. Leaves basal, deeply 3-parted, and the segments again lobed into linear parts. Sepals 5, green, and hairy; petals 2–5, yellow, ¹/₄–¹/₂" long, and hairy. Seeds hairy. WEEDY, PJ.

Early spring–early summer.

Comments: *Ranunculus* (small frog) refers to many of the plants in this genus that grow in moist locations. Presence of Bur Buttercup indicates a disturbed site.

Bur Buttercup

BLACKBRUSH
Coleogyne ramosissima
Rose Family (Rosaceae)

Description: Rounded shrubs up to 4' tall, with dense branches that may be spiny at the tip. Narrow, inversely lance-shaped leaves opposite, evergreen, up to ³/₈" long, and with a small point at the tip. Flowers about ¹/₂" across, with 4 yellowish sepals (brownish beneath); may lack petals entirely or have up to 4; with many stamens. Fruit a small egg-shaped seed; the woody sepals may persist. Blk, WDS.

Midspring–early summer.

Comments: Blackbrush plants form vast plant communities throughout the Canyonlands region. *Ramosissima* (many branched) refers to the intricate branching habit of the shrub. Branches darken when wet, hence the common name.

Blackbrush

Golden Currant

GOLDEN CURRANT
Ribes aureum
Saxifrage Family (Saxifragaceae)

Description: Shrubs, 3–9' tall, with smooth, thornless branchlets. Leaf blades rounded to kidney-shaped, ³/₈–3" wide, and 3-lobed, the lobes again lobed or toothed. Five petal-like, yellow sepals; petals smaller and yellow or reddish. Berries smooth, black, red, orange, or translucent golden. RIP, PJ, CDS.

Midspring–early summer.

Comments: *Ribes* is from the Arabic *ribas* (acid-tasting), in reference to the edible but tart fruit.

PINK AND PURPLE FLOWERS

*This section includes flowers
ranging from pink to purple or shades
in between. Some bluish plants may be in
this section, but be sure to also check
the blue flower section.*

JONES CYCLADENIA
Cycladenia humilis
Dogbane Family (Apocynaceae)

Description: Perennial, 4–12" tall, with smooth stems. Main leaves $1^1/_4$–$3^3/_4$" long, oval to rounded, and tapering to a broad petiole at the base. Flower stems bear 2–8 flowers, each with 5 green calyx lobes and a funnel-shaped, rose-purple corolla, $3/_4$" long. MDS, PJ.

Midspring–early summer.

Comments: A federally listed threatened species that grows on gypsum-bearing, saline soils. *Humilis* (low) refers to the stature of the plant.

Jones Cycladenia

Showy Milkweed

SHOWY MILKWEED
Asclepias speciosa
Milkweed Family (Asclepiadaceae)

Description: Stout, 3–6' tall unbranched perennial with milky sap. Stem and undersides of leaves may be covered with dense white hairs. Leaves opposite and oval, 1–6" across and $2^1/_4$–8" long. Flowers in rounded clusters that hang from short, stout stalks. Flowers over 1" wide with 5 rose-purple petals and 5 pinkish cream, needlelike, pouch-shaped hoods. Pods 3–5" long, spiny or smooth. RIP, WEEDY.

Late spring–summer.

Comments: Monarch butterfly larvae consume the toxic foliage of this plant, which makes this insect less palatable to predators. The silky down of the seedpods, which is 5 or 6 times more buoyant than cork, was used to stuff pillows and, during World War II, life jackets and flight suits. *Speciosa* means this is the common species of the genus.

Russian Knapweed

RUSSIAN KNAPWEED
Centaurea repens
Sunflower Family (Asteraceae)

Description: Perennial, 1–3' tall, with cob-webby hairs or smooth stems. Basal leaves withered when flowers bloom; narrow stem leaves ³/₈–2¹/₂" long and may be toothed along the margin. Outer bracts beneath the flower heads broad. Flower heads ³/₈–1" wide and urn-shaped; disk flowers tubular and pink or purplish. WEEDY, RIP.

Late spring–midsummer.

Comments: Introduced noxious weed from Eurasia, now widely established in North America. *Repens* (creeping) refers to the plant's habit of spreading by underground roots.

RYDBERG'S THISTLE
Cirsium rydbergii
Sunflower Family (Asteraceae)

Description: Perennial herbaceous plants with the lower part of stem covered with brown leaf bases. Huge basal leaves, 1–3' long and 6–18" wide, doubly lobed, and the lobes narrow or wide. Spines along the leaf edges are up to ³/₈" long. Stems 2–4' tall, with the stem leaves smooth and smaller upwards. Flower heads ³/₈–³/₄" high and ³/₈–1¹/₈" wide. Outer bracts below the heads abruptly end in downward curved spines. Flowers pink. HG.

Midspring–midsummer.

Comments: The huge basal rosettes, tall flowering stems, and small heads make this thistle relatively easy to identify. *Rydbergii* honors Per Axel Rydberg (1860–1931), an American botanist who was an authority on western plants.

Rydberg's Thistle

SHOWY RUSHPINK
Lygodesmia grandiflora
Sunflower Family (Asteraceae)

Description: Perennial, with stems 2–20" tall and slender branches. Leaves alternate, $^1/_4$–4" long, and mostly linear to lance-shaped. Flower heads cylindrical with 5–10 pink or pinkish purple to lavender-blue ray flowers that are $^3/_4$–1$^1/_2$" long. Pappus has finely barbed bristles. MDS, PJ.

Late spring–early summer.

Comments: *Lygodesmia* is from the Greek *lygos* (pliant) and *desmia* (bundle) in reference to the clustered stems, which are very pliant and twiglike. *Grandiflora* (large flower) refers to the size of the showy flowers.

Showy Rushpink

TANSYLEAF ASTER
Machaeranthera tanacetifolia
Sunflower Family (Asteraceae)

Description: Herbaceous annual, 3–20" tall, and with glandular or long, soft hairs. Leaves $^3/_8$–2$^1/_2$" long, highly dissected to the midrib, with each segment ending in a small, spiny bristle. Flower heads $^3/_8$" high, $^3/_8$–$^3/_4$" wide, with bracts lance-shaped to linear. Ray flowers 11–23, pink-purple or blue-purple, and surrounding a central cluster of yellow disk flowers. Blk, MDS, PJ.

Summer–Early Autumn.

Comments: *Machaeranthera* (sickle anther) refers to the shape of the anthers. *Tanacetifolia* (tansylike leaves) refers to the fernlike leaves, which make this an easy aster to identify. Two other common *Machaeranthera* are *M. canescens*, Hoary Aster, and *M. bigelowii*, Bigelow's Aster.

Tansyleaf Aster

Annual Wirelettuce

ANNUAL WIRELETTUCE
Stephanomeria exigua
Sunflower Family (Asteraceae)

Description: Annual or biennial, with herbage smooth or covered with fine hairs. Slender, wiry stems grow erect, 2–24" tall. Main leaves deeply divided to the midline, with the lobes sometimes divided again. Upper leaves few and smaller. Flower heads ¹/₂" wide with pink to white ray flowers only; the rays are toothed at their tips. WDS, MDS, StDS, PJ. *Spring–late summer.*

Comments: *Stephanomeria* (crown divided) refers to the spaces between the ray flowers. *Exigua* refers to the milky latex that is exuded from the plant. This plant is a relative of cultivated lettuce and its bitter leaves may be eaten.

AFRICAN MUSTARD
Malcolmia africana
Mustard Family (Brassicaceae)

Description: Annual, with stems 1–16" tall or low growing and covered with forked or 3-rayed hairs. Leaves mainly basal, ¹/₂–3¹/₂" long, inversely lance-shaped or elliptical, and toothed along the margin. Flowers ¹/₄–¹/₂" wide with 4 pink to lavender petals and 4 reddish purple sepals. Seedpods straight and 1–3" long. WEEDY. *Spring.*

Comments: *Malcolmia* is for William Malcolm (1778–1805), a British horticulturist. *Africana* is for this exotic weed's home continent—Africa.

RAVEN TENNYSON

African Mustard

Rockcress

ROCKCRESS
Arabis pulchra
Mustard Family (Brassicaceae)

Description: Perennial, to 2' tall; stems have fine, branching hairs throughout or are smooth above. Basal leaves arranged in poorly developed rosettes; leaves are $^3/_8$–$2^3/_8$" long, narrow, and inversely lance- or spatula-shaped. Flowers $^1/_2$" wide with 4 pale pink to white petals. Thin pods, up to $2^1/_2$" long, curve downwards at maturity. MDS, PJ.

Midspring–early summer.

Comments: *Arabis* (from Arabia) denotes where a member of this genus was first described. Pretty Rockcress, *A. perennans,* has smaller purple flowers.

Whipple's Fishhook

WHIPPLE'S FISHHOOK
Sclerocactus whipplei
Cactus Family (Cactaceae)

Description: Solitary or occasionally small colonies of cylindrical or circular plants, the stems mostly 2–14" tall and up to 6" in diameter. Main spines are ³/₈–3" long and most are hooked at the tip like a fishhook. Flowers mainly pink, white, or yellow and up to 2" long. StDS, MDS, CDS, PJ.

Spring–early summer.

Comments: Named for Amiel Wicks Whipple (1818–1863), a topographical engineer who served on a boundary survey between the United States and Mexico in 1853–1856 and was the leader of the Pacific Railroad Survey on the 35th Parallel. Some specimens may have straight spines and/or variously colored flowers.

LONG-FLOWER SNOWBERRY
Symphoricarpos longiflorus
Honeysuckle Family (Caprifoliaceae)

Description: Woody shrub to 3' tall; young stems either smooth or covered with fine, soft hairs. Opposite leaves oval or lance-shaped and $^1/_2$" long. Flowers solitary or in pairs, growing in the angle between the leaf and the stem. Slender corolla tube, $^1/_4$–$^3/_4$" long, is blue to deep pink and flares open at the mouth. Fruit is a white, 2-seeded berry. MDS, PJ.

Late spring–early summer.

Comments: *Symphoricarpos* is from the Greek *syn* (together), *phorein* (to bear), and *karpos* (fruit), referring to the closely clustered, snow-white fruits. *Longiflorus* means "long flower."

JOEL S. TUHY

Long-Flower Snowberry

Greasewood

GREASEWOOD
Sarcobatus vermiculatus
Goosefoot Family (Chenopodiaceae)

Description: Thorny shrubs 3–7' tall, with white bark and linear, succulent leaves $^1/_4$–$1^3/_4$" long. Male and female flowers separate but found on the same plant. Rose-colored male flowers arranged spirally along a short, often upright spike; female flowers fewer but also arranged along a short spike in the axils of leaves. Seeds are cup-shaped below a papery wing. StDS.

Midspring–summer.

Comments: Grows in alkaline soils; sodium or potassium salts often accumulate in or on the leaves. *Sarcobatus* is from the Greek *sarco* (flesh) and *batos* (bramble), referring to the succulent leaves and spiny branches. The tough wood was used for tools or firewood.

JOEL S. TUHY

Crescent Milkvetch

CRESCENT MILKVETCH
Astragalus amphioxys
Pea Family (Fabaceae)

Description: Low-growing perennial. Compound leaves up to 1¹/₂" long with 5–21 elliptical or egg-shaped leaflets per leaf. Leaves and stems covered with soft grayish hairs. Leafless flowering stalks, ³/₄–8" tall, bear 2–13 flowers near the tip. Purplish pink flowers ¹/₂–1" long; calyx tubular and the upper 2 petals fused together forming a hood. Lower 3 petals are small and overlapping. Crescent-shaped pods are smooth and 1¹/₂" long. Blk, StDS, CDS, PJ.

Spring.

Comments: Crescent Milkvetch, named for the shape of the seedpods, blooms early in the spring.

PAINTED MILKVETCH
Astragalus ceramicus
Pea Family (Fabaceae)

Description: Perennial, with stems sprawling to erect, 1–16" long, and covered with pick-shaped hairs. Leaves compound, ³/₄–6" long; leaflets 3–13, ¹/₄–1" long, and threadlike. Flower stalks with 2-15 dull purple or pink flowers, ¹/₄–¹/₂" long. Pods inflated, elliptical, and with reddish mottling. PJ, SDS, RIP.

Midspring–late spring.

Comments: Grows in sandy locations; *ceramicus* refers to the pod's potterylike appearance.

Painted Milkvetch

RIMROCK MILKVETCH
Astragalus desperatus
Pea Family (Fabaceae)

Description: Low-growing perennial, $1/2$–$4^1/2$" tall. Compound leaves $1/2$–$4^1/2$" long with 7–17 elliptical or inversely lance-shaped leaflets. Main flower stalk up to 5" tall; individual flowers arise on short stems. Calyx tube may be $1/2$" long and bell-shaped; pink-purple or two-toned petals are $1/4$" long. Seedpods elliptical or curved, up to $3/4$" long, and covered with stiff hairs. MDS, PJ.

Spring–summer.

Comments: *Astragalus* is the Greek name for *legume*, which may be derived from *astragalos* (ankle bone), in reference to the shape of the leaves or pods. A Colorado Plateau endemic.

Rimrock Milkvetch

Woolly Locoweed

WOOLLY LOCOWEED
Astragalus mollissimus
Pea Family (Fabaceae)

Description: Perennial, from a very short stem or none at all, 2–34" tall. Compound leaves $3/4$–11" long with 15–35 woolly, elliptical to egg-shaped leaflets. Flower stalks $3/4$–10" long, purplish, and densely covered with hairs. Flowers 7–20 per stalk; calyx is $1/4$–$1/2$" long, hairy, and with 5 pointed teeth. Flowers $3/4$" long, pink-purple or bicolored with some white, with the upper petal flaring at the end. Egg-shaped seedpods, $1/3$–1" long, are densely hairy. StDS, MDS, PJ.

Early spring–summer.

Comments: *Mollissimus* (most soft) refers to the dense hairy covering of the leaves and stems, which also inspires the common name. Plants contain an alkaloid, locoine, which can cause livestock to "go loco," or even die, if they eat too much of this species.

Preuss' Milkvetch

HERONSBILL
Erodium cicutarium
Geranium Family (Geraniaceae)

Description: Stems low growing or prostrate, usually 2–5" long, and covered with small, stiff hairs that are sticky. Leaves up to 4¹/₂" long and fernlike; each of the deeply divided leaflets is irregularly lobed or toothed. Bright pink flowers, ¹/₄–¹/₂" across, are borne in small clusters. Elongated fruit tapers like a bird's beak. WEEDY.

Spring–midautumn.

Comments: Introduced from the Mediterranean region and noted in Utah in 1844 by John C. Frémont. The auger-shaped seeds "burrow" into the soil with the help of the long seed tail. *Erodium* is from the Greek *erodios* (heron), referring to the shape of the fruit; *cicutarium* (like *Cicuta*) refers to the resemblance of the leaves to Water-Hemlock, *Cicuta maculata.*

PREUSS' MILKVETCH
Astragalus preussii
Pea Family (Fabaceae)

Description: Perennial or annual, stems 4–15" long, reddish, and growing upright from a woody base. Compound leaves 1¹/₂–5" long; the 7–25 elliptical to rounded, smooth leaflets 3/4" long. Flowers 3–22 per stalk; small, green, 5-toothed calyx subtends the tubular set of petals. Upper petal large and flares at the tip. Flowers are pinkish purple, white, or bicolored and about ³/₄" long. Pods elliptical, smooth or covered with soft hairs, ³/₄" long, and become papery or leathery upon drying. Blk, MDS.

Spring.

Comments: Preuss' Milkvetch prefers selenium-bearing soils and may be toxic to livestock. Named for Charles Preuss (1803–1854), a talented scientist and cartographer on three of Freemont's expeditions.

Heronsbill

SCORPIONWEED
Phacelia crenulata
Waterleaf Family (Hydrophyllaceae)

Description: Annual, 2–32" tall. Leaves basal, strap-shaped to elliptical, with the margins deeply lobed or wavy. Sticky, glandular hairs mixed with nonglandular hairs along the leaves and stems. Flowers along an elongated axis that curls like a scorpion's tail. Blue-violet to purple flowers are ¼" long, bell-shaped, and the stamens and style protrude above the flower. CDS, StDS, PJ.

Spring–summer.

Comments: *Phacelia* is from the Greek *phakelos* (fascicle), referring to the clustered flowers. *Crenulata* (shallow, rounded teeth) refers to the leaf margin. Foliage is strong smelling.

Scorpionweed

GARY N. SALAMACHA

Purple Sage

PURPLE SAGE
Poliomintha incana
Mint Family (Lamiaceae)

Description: Woody shrubs, 12–40" tall, with rounded or square stems. Opposite linear leaves, ³/₈–1¹/₈" long, are covered with dense white hairs. Flowers borne in upper leaf axils; corolla is 2-lipped, ½" long, and lavender to whitish with purple dots on the lower lip. Blk, SDS, MDS, PJ.

Midspring–summer.

Comments: *Poliomintha* means "gray mint," a reference to the plant's gray-looking leaves. The flowers are used as a seasoning. The calyx has a purplish cast that gives the plant its name.

Prairie Wild Onion

PRAIRIE WILD ONION
Allium textile
Lily Family (Liliaceae)

Description: Perennial, with a buried $3/4$"-thick bulb. Threadlike leaves, 2–4 per flowering stalk; leaves can be up to 9" long. Leafless flowering stalk, 1–9" long, bearing round cluster of 5–54 flowers. Three sepals and 3 petals are white or pale pink with deep purple nectar guides. Fruit is a small capsule. StDS, MDS, PJ.

Spring–early summer.

Comments: *Allium* (to avoid) refers to the odor and flavor of the edible bulbs. *Textile* (textile or fabric) refers to the dark brown, fabric-like fibers that loosely encase the bulb.

TRAILING FOUR O'CLOCK
Allionia incarnata
Four O'Clock Family (Nyctaginaceae)

Description: Perennial, with stems growing along the ground, 4–36" long, radiating from a central root crown. Leaves and stems have sticky hairs. Leaves opposite but unequal in length, $3/8$–$1^1/8$" long, and egg-shaped to elliptical. Magenta to pink-purple flowers are $1/4$–$3/4$" long and lack true petals. Blk, SDS, StDS.

Midspring–early autumn.

Comments: Flowers open in the afternoon, hence the common name "four o'clock."

Trailing Four O'Clock

SHOWY FOUR O'CLOCK
Mirabilis multiflora
Four O'Clock Family (Nyctaginaceae)

Description: Perennial clump-forming plant, mainly 1–3' tall and as broad or broader. Opposite, short-petioled leaves are rounded to egg-shaped, ³/₄–7" long, and may be pointed at the tip. Flowers in small clusters in leaf axils; individual magenta flowers 1¹/₂–2¹/₄" long and funnel-shaped. Blk, PJ.

Late spring–summer.

Comments: *Mirabilis* (marvelous) and *multiflora* (many-flowered) describe this beautiful plant. The flowers open in the late afternoon—not necessarily at four o'clock sharp, however.

Showy Four O'Clock

Cave Primrose

CAVE PRIMROSE
Primula specuicola
Primrose Family (Primulaceae)

Description: Perennial, 2–11" long, with withered leaves at the base of the plant. Leaves ³/₄–8" long, spatula-shaped to elliptical, variously toothed along the margins, and white-mealy below, greener above. Lavender to pink flowers with the corolla tube rimmed in yellow are ¹/₂–²/₃" wide and in clusters at the end of a leafless stalk. HG.

Late winter–spring.

Comments: A Colorado Plateau endemic; plant blooms around Easter, hence another common name, Easter Flower. *Primula* is a diminutive of *primus* (first), another reference to the plant's blooming in early spring.

WOODS' ROSE
Rosa woodsii
Rose Family (Rosaceae)

Description: Shrubs to 7' tall; stems armed with spines or prickles. Compound leaves; 3–9 leaflets have toothed margins and are ¹/₂–4" long. Pinkish flowers solitary or in small clusters; each flower ¹/₂–2" wide. Fruits are red-orange to yellow and mealy. RIP, PJ.
Midspring–summer depending upon elevation.

Comments: *Rosa* is the classical Latin name. Fruits edible although seedy. Petals from the cultivated rose, *R. gallica,* provide the rose oil used in perfumes.

Woods' Rose

WRIGHT'S BIRDSBEAK
Cordylanthus wrightii
Figwort Family (Scrophulariaceae)

Description: Annual, with stems 6–36" tall and much branched. Leaves ³/₈–1¹/₈" long, often 3- to 5-lobed into narrow segments. Flowers, ¹/₂–1" long, with 3- to 5-lobed bracts beneath the yellow to purple 2-lipped corolla. Corolla lips unequal in length. Blk, StDS, MDS, PJ.
Midsummer–fall.

Comments: *Cordylanthus* is from the Greek *kordyle* (club) and *anthos* (flower), referring to the shape of the flowers. The common name was inspired by the corolla's overlapping and unequal pair of lips, which resemble a bird's beak.

Wright's Birdsbeak

PINYON-JUNIPER LOUSEWORT
Pedicularis centranthera
Figwort Family (Scrophulariaceae)

Description: Perennial, with stems 1½–2¾" tall. Leaves divided to the midrib, 2–6" long, linear to lance-shaped, and with "ruffled" toothed edges with white tips. Flowers in tight clusters; 5 lobes of calyx of unequal lengths and slightly hairy. Corolla purple or yellowish, ¾" long, and 2-lipped, the upper lip hooded and the lower lip 3-lobed. PJ.

Late spring–midsummer.

Comments: *Pedicularis* (of lice) refers to the ancient use of the seeds to destroy lice. In a sort of irony, the plants are partially parasitic on other plants.

Pinyon-Juniper Lousewort

Palmer's Penstemon

PALMER'S PENSTEMON
Penstemon palmerii
Figwort Family (Scrophulariaceae)

Description: Perennial with clustered stems, 2–5' tall. Thick leaves ¾–4½" long, elliptical, and smooth. Flowers pink to creamy white, inflated, with prominent wine-red nectar guidelines on the inside of the lower lip and a prominent yellow "beard." MDS, PJ, CDS.

Midspring–summer.

Comments: One of the stamens is "bearded," which gives the plant another common name: "beardtongue." The plant's inflated flowers indicate that bees and other insects, and also hummingbirds, pollinate this species. *Palmerii* is for Edward Palmer (1831–1911), an English immigrant who collected many native American bird and plant specimens in the West.

GREEN AND/OR TINY FLOWERS

*This section includes both green flowers and
the tiny, non-showy, and/or unisexual
flowers of some of the tree species.*

BOXELDER
Acer negundo
Maple Family (Aceraceae)

Description: Medium-sized, many-branched tree, 12–38' tall. Branchlets smooth or velvet-hairy. Leaves opposite and compound with 3–7 coarsely toothed or lobed leaflets. Leaflets ³/₄–4" long, terminal leaflet long-stemmed. Male and female flowers borne separately in drooping tassels on separate trees. Fruit is a double-winged seed. RIP.

Spring.

Comments: Boxelder is both from the "boxing" or tapping of the tree by settlers for its low-grade syrup and from the leaves' resemblance to those of the Elderberry. *Acer* is Latin for "maple."

Boxelder

Pallid Milkweed

PALLID MILKWEED
Asclepias cryptoceras
Milkweed Family (Asclepiadaceae)

Description: Plant 4–12" long, stems trailing along the ground. Opposite leaves are smooth and broadly oval, almost as long as broad. Flower clusters may or may not be short-stalked; individual flowers have greenish white petals that are bent downward, and each lobe is about ¹/₂" long. The 5 pouch-shaped hoods are pale rose. Seedpods are broadly spindle-shaped and up to 2³/₄" long. Blk, StDS, CDS, PJ.

Midspring–late spring.

Comments: *Asclepias* refers to Asklepios, a human physician who was an authority on the medicinal properties of plants and who, according to Greek myth, could return the dead to life. Hades, the god of the dead, feared a loss of "employment" and coerced his brother Zeus into killing Asklepios with a thunderbolt.

Dwarf Milkweed

DWARF MILKWEED
Asclepias macrosperma
Milkweed Family (Asclepiadaceae)

Description: Plant 2–10" long; the stems mostly recline along the ground. Stems and leaves densely covered with hairs. Short-stemmed, opposite leaves egg-shaped and somewhat narrowly pointed at the end, and often folded longitudinally in half. Flower clusters located at the ends of the stems; 5 petals greenish white and bent downwards, and 5 greenish white pouch-shaped sacs. Seedpods spindle-shaped, 1^1/$_2$–2^1/$_2$" long, and mostly smooth. MDS, Blk, CDS, PJ.

Midspring–early summer.

Comments: *Macrosperma* (large seed) is in reference to the size of the pods and seeds. Asklepios, a Greek physician, used a symbol of 1 or 2 serpents entwined about a staff, the caduceus, which is still the symbol for the medical profession today.

BUR RAGWEED
Ambrosia acanthicarpa
Sunflower Family (Asteraceae)

Description: Annual to 3' tall, but often branching from the base and with the stems reclining along the ground. Alternate leaves ^{3}/$_8$–1^3/$_4$" long, lobed; often the lobes are deeply divided. Numerous tiny, inconspicuous, drab flowers are borne along an elongated axis and are oriented downward. Male flowers are separate from female flowers, male flowers located above. Seeds covered with 2–3 series of flattened, curved spines. WEEDY.

Summer–autumn.

Comments: *Ambrosia* in Greek mythology was the food of the gods; here, it refers to the sweet smell of this non-native plant, which is a major contributor to hay fever.

Bur Ragweed

OLD MAN SAGE
Artemisia filifolia
Sunflower Family (Asteraceae)

Description: Silvery or grayish, highly branched shrub, 2–3' or taller. Threadlike leaves covered with small, dense hairs. Dense plumes of tiny, bell-shaped flowers form clusters that hang downward. Seeds are smooth and minute. SDS, Blk, MDS, PJ, WDS.

Midsummer–autumn.

Comments: Silvery leaves, wispy foliage, and beardlike look of the dense flower clusters give this plant its common name. *Artemisia* is from Artemisia, the wife of Mausolus, who was the ancient ruler of Caria (Southwest Asia Minor). Artemisia was named in honor of Artemis, the Greek virgin goddess of the hunt and of wild nature. *Filifolia* means "threadlike leaves."

Old Man Sage

Longleaf Brickellbush

LONGLEAF BRICKELLBUSH
Brickellia longifolia
Sunflower Family (Asteraceae)

Description: Densely branched shrub, 3–6' tall. Alternate, stalkless leaves, $3/8–4^3/4$" long, narrow, and gradually tapering to a point. Flowers 3–5 per cluster, with many clusters borne along an elongated stalk at the apex of the branch. Outer bracts below the flower cluster teardrop-shaped, while the inner ones are long and slender. Small green flower heads bear only disk flowers; the dried flowering stalks may overwinter. RIP, HG.

Summer–midautumn.

Comments: The genus is named for John Brickell (1749–1809), a physician and botanist from Savannah, Georgia. *Longifolia* means "long leaves."

Water Birch

WATER BIRCH
Betula occidentalis
Birch Family (Betulaceae)

Description: Small tree or dense shrub to 20' tall; may have several main trunks. Bark reddish or yellowish brown, shiny, and marked with horizontal rows of thin holes. Leaves broad and egg-shaped, $1/2$–$3^1/2$" long, with an abrupt point at the tip and doubly toothed margins. Unisexual flowers grow separately on the same plant; both arranged in dense, hanging clusters. Fruit is a papery, conelike structure with tiny seeds. RIP.

Early–midspring.

Comments: *Occidentalis* (western) refers to this plant's geographical distribution in the western United States. Grows in moist locations.

HALOGETON
Halogeton glomeratus
Goosefoot Family (Chenopodiaceae)

Description: Annual, 1–20" tall. Alternate leaves fleshy, $1/4$–$3/4$" long, and with a slender spine at the tip. Small membranous flowers borne in leaf axils. Egg-shaped bracts below the flowers. StDS, MDS, PJ.

Summer.

Comments: First introduced into northern Nevada in the early 1930s as an experimental forage crop (it failed, as it was too high in oxalates and therefore toxic to livestock); nevertheless, the plant quickly spread into the lower deserts of Nevada and Utah. *Halogeton* is from the Greek *halos* (salt) and *geiton* (neighbor); the plants grow well in saline soils.

Halogeton

RUSSIAN-THISTLE
Salsola pestifer
Goosefoot Family (Chenopodiaceae)

Description: Annual with red-purple stems to 3' or taller; plants often branch near the base, and the stems grow erect or curve upwards. Narrow, linear leaves ¹/₂–2¹/₄" long, spine-tipped, and smaller and more spinelike towards the top. Tiny flowers in short clusters and spiny; fruit with papery disk surrounding the seed. WEEDY.

Late spring–early summer.

Comments: First introduced into South Dakota around 1873 from Eurasia, the plant spread over the American West in a few decades. When the plant dies, the roots break off in the soil; as the detached plant "tumbles" in the wind ("tumbleweed" is another common name), it breaks apart and spreads the seeds. Young shoots are edible; *salsola* means "salty," referring to the taste of the young leaves. *Pestifer* (pest) is a reference to this plant's bad reputation.

Russian-Thistle

Utah Juniper

UTAH JUNIPER
Juniperus osteosperma
Cypress Family (Cupressaceae)

Description: Shrub or small tree with thin, fibrous bark that becomes shredded with age. Leaves opposite or in whorls of threes, overlapping and scalelike, up to ¹/₄" long, and slightly toothed along the margin. Juvenile plant's leaves bluish green and lance-shaped. Male and female cones borne separately on the same plant; seeds enclosed in a hard shell within a bluish gray waxy coating. RIP, WDS, CDS, PJ.

Spring.

Comments: One of the two primary members of the pinyon-juniper plant community, which is a major and widespread habitat type in the Southwest. *Juniperus* is the Latin name for "juniper" and *osteosperma* means "hard seed." The female cones resemble a hard berry.

Mormon Tea

MORMON TEA
Ephedra viridis
Ephedra Family (Ephedraceae)

Description: Shrub 4–60" tall, with upright branches mainly bright green and smooth. Small, scalelike leaves, located at the stem joints, in pairs or sometimes in whorls. Male cones 2 or more, inversely egg-shaped, and $^1/_4$" long. Female cones inversely egg-shaped, up to $^3/_8$" long, and with 4-8 pairs of rounded bracts. Brown seeds borne in pairs. Blk, StDS, CDS, PJ.

Spring-early summer.

Comments: Steeping the branchlets makes a noncaffeinated tea that is used to treat colds and congestion. The commercial drug ephedrine (which is named after the genus) comes from *E. chinensis*, which grows in China. *Viridis* means "green," referring to the plant's overall color.

GAMBEL'S OAK
Quercus gambelii
Beech Family (Fagaceae)

Description: Deciduous shrub or small tree, to 30' tall, often growing in groves. Young leaves have dense star-shaped hairs on both sides, becoming, with age, greener and smooth above and hairy below. Leaf size from $^3/_4$–7"; individual leaves are elliptical or egg-shaped in outline and deeply lobed. Male and female flowers borne separately in dense hanging clusters. Acorns $^1/_2$–$^3/_4$" long. RIP, PJ.

Spring.

Comments: Plants may propagate by cloning of underground stems. Native Americans collected the acorns, ground the nuts into flour, and soaked it in water to remove the bitter tannins. *Quercus* is Latin for "oak." *Gambelii* honors William Gambel (1821–1849), an assistant curator at the Natural Academy of Sciences (now called the National Academy of Sciences) and an avid western plant collector.

Gambel's Oak

SHINNERY OAK
Quercus havardii
Beech Family (Fagaceae)

Description: Deciduous shrub 2–6' tall. Young leaves densely hairy on both sides, becoming smoother with age. Leaves $^1/_2$–$2^1/_2$" long, elliptical or inversely lance-shaped, and often with 6–10 toothed lobes along the margin; lobes may be pointed or toothed again. Male and female flowers borne separately in dense clusters that hang downwards. Acorns $^1/_2$–$^3/_4$" long. SDS, Blk, PJ.

Spring.

Comments: Complex root systems of the Shinnery Oak help stabilize sandy soils. Formerly called "Wavy-Leaf Oak."

Shinnery Oak

WHITE-MARGINED SWERTIA
Swertia albomarginata
Gentian Family (Gentianaceae)

Description: Perennial, 2–3' tall, with smooth, opposite, branching stems. Leaves opposite or in whorls of 4, white-margined, $1^1/_2$–4" long, and linear or inversely lance-shaped. Greenish white flowers have 4 petals and sepals; the petals have greenish dots and their lobes have a solitary gland that is fringed with short, soft, white hairs. WDS, CDS, PJ.

Midspring–early summer.

Comments: *Swertia* is for Emanuel Sweert, a sixteenth-century Dutch gardener and author. *Albomarginata* (white margin) refers to the conspicuous white edge of the leaf.

White-Margined Swertia

Showy Gentian

SHOWY GENTIAN
Swertia radiata
Gentian Family (Gentianaceae)

Description: Perennial, often 4–6' tall. Basal leaves spatula-shaped or elliptical, 8–20" long, and smooth or slightly hairy. Stem leaves smaller and lance-shaped or inversely lance-shaped. Flowers borne in whorled clusters; each flower $^3/_8$–$^3/_4$" wide with purplish dots on the greenish petals and 2 glands on each petal's lobe. CDS, PJ.

Late spring–summer.

Comments: Also called "elkweed." Navajos used to rub a cold tea made from the leaves on the bodies of hunters and horses to strengthen them for long expeditions. Dried leaves were mixed with tobacco and smoked.

COYOTE BUSH
Forestiera pubescens
Olive Family (Oleaceae)

Description: Sprawling deciduous shrub, 6' or taller. Inversely lance-shaped or elliptical leaves $^1/_2$–2" long and sometimes with small serrations along the margin. Uni- or bisexual, inconspicuous flowers, with yellowish stamens, are borne on the same plant often before the leaves mature. Fruit is a blue-black fleshy fruit that encases a hard seed. RIP.

Midspring.

Comments: Fruits are eaten by foxes and coyotes, hence its common name. Grows in moist locations, especially along riverbanks. Also called New Mexico Privet.

Coyote Bush

SINGLELEAF ASH
Fraxinus anomala
Olive Family (Oleaceae)

Description: Deciduous shrub or small tree, 4–13' tall. Smooth leaves $1/2$–$1 1/2$" long, egg-shaped, and slightly toothed or serrated along the margin. Tiny flowers lack petals, have orange anthers, and are borne in dense clusters in the leaf axils. Each seed has one papery wing. Blk, MDS, PJ.

Spring.

Comments: The stout wood was used for tool handles and digging sticks by settlers and Native Americans. *Anomala* (anomaly) refers to this unique species of ash that has single, not compound, leaves.

Singleleaf Ash

Helleborine

HELLEBORINE
Epipactis gigantea
Orchid Family (Orchidaceae)

Description: Smooth, stout stems, 5–15", with a tinge of purple at the base. Egg-shaped or elliptical leaves are broadest on the lower portion of the stem, narrower above, and 2–8" long. Showy flowers, $1/2$–$3/4$" wide, have greenish to rose-colored sepals with purple or dull red veins. Petals brownish purple; the lower one is saclike and strongly marked with red or purple veins. Fruit is an elliptical capsule that hangs downward. RIP, HG.

Midspring–midsummer.

Comments: Grows in moist sites along streams, in meadows, or in hanging gardens. *Epipactis* is Greek for "hellebore," a different type of orchid.

Alcove Bog-Orchid

ALCOVE BOG-ORCHID
Habenaria zothecina
Orchid Family (Orchidaceae)

Description: Perennial, 7–24" tall. Leaves elliptical or narrowly linear and long. Flowering stalk bears 5–20 green or yellowish green flowers. Upper sepal is in close contact with the petals and forms a hood over the style. Lateral sepals curved and the petals triangularly lance-shaped. The lower petal (or "lip") is yellowish and linear. HG, RIP.

Late spring–midsummer.

Comments: A Colorado Plateau endemic that grows in moist locations along streams and seeps and in hanging gardens. *Habenaria* is from Latin *habena* (reins or narrow strap), in reference to the narrow lip of the lower petal in some of the species.

PINYON
Pinus edulis
Pine Family (Pinaceae)

Description: Small- to medium-sized trees, mainly 15–45' tall. Yellowish brown bark is thin and scaly, becoming furrowed and grayer with age. Evergreen needles mostly 2 per cluster, ³/₈–2" long, rigid, and sharply pointed. Male cones ¹/₈" long; resin-covered female cones oval and up to 2" long. Seeds brown to tan, thick-shelled, and wingless. CDS, PJ, RIP.

Summer.

Comments: One of the two dominant trees of the pinyon-juniper plant community, it is the state tree of New Mexico. *Pinus* is the Latin name for "pine" and *edulis* (edible) refers to the highly nutritive seeds. The sticky resin was used to waterproof Native American baskets and pots, glue feathers to arrows, and a host of other uses, some still in practice today.

Pinyon

CANAIGRE
Rumex hymenosepalus
Buckwheat Family (Polygonaceae)

Description: Perennial, with stout stems 8–40" tall that arise from a cluster of deeply buried thick roots. Lower leaves with long stems; blades 3–10" long, elliptical to lance-shaped, fleshy, and twisted or curled. Stem leaves smaller. Compact cluster of flowers borne at the stem tip; the 6 similar floral segments are green to red. Three inner segments become enlarged, forming pinkish papery wings (as shown in the photograph) on the fruit. Blk, MDS, SDS.

Spring–early summer.

Comments: Also called "wild rhubarb"; the leaves were eaten as greens and the stems cooked like rhubarb. *Hymenosepalus* (membranous sepals) refers to the 3 inner segments that become papery when the plant is in fruit.

Canaigre

Large-Valve Dock

LARGE-VALVE DOCK
Rumex venosus
Buckwheat Family (Polygonaceae)

Description: Perennial propagates from horizontally spreading roots, stems 4–20" tall. Stem leaves egg-shaped to elliptical, $3/4$–$5^1/2$" long, and $3/8$–2" wide. Flowers numerous; greenish floral segments $1/4$" long; 3 of the segments become enlarged and red in fruit (as shown in photograph). SDS.

Midspring–early summer.

Comments: *Venosus* (veined) refers to the prominent leaf veins. "Large-valve" refers to the large wings on the seeds. Boiling the roots produces red, yellow, or black dyes, depending upon the material added to the roots. A poultice from mashed roots has been used to treat burns.

Dwarf Mountain-Mahogany

DWARF MOUNTAIN-MAHOGANY
Cercocarpus intricatus
Rose Family (Rosaceae)

Description: Shrub, 1¹/₂–7' tall and intricately branched. Evergreen leaves ¹/₈–³/₄" long; narrow and linear; smooth or with short, appressed, stiff hairs; and with margins rolling inwards. Tiny flowers about ¹/₈" long or smaller, lacking petals, and solitary or in small clusters. Seeds have an elongated tail. CDS, PJ.
Midspring.

Comments: *Cercocarpus* is from the Greek *kerkos* (tail) and *carpos* (fruit), referring to the long feathery tails. *C. montanus,* the Alder-Leaf Mountain Mahogany, has deciduous leaves that resemble those of an alder, but has fruits similar to *C. intricatus.*

FREMONT'S COTTONWOOD
Populus fremontii
Willow Family (Salicaceae)

Description: Trees to 75' tall; mature trees with broad, rounded crowns. Bark smooth and whitish on young trees, deeply furrowed and grayish or brown on older trunks. Leaves triangular or heart-shaped, variously toothed along the margin, and with long petioles. Male and female flowers borne separately on the same tree in short clusters that appear before the leaves in spring. Seeds covered with fine white hairs. RIP.
Midspring–early summer.

Comments: Named after the explorer John C. Frémont (1813–1890). Cottonwood seeds disperse after the spring runoff; seeds germinate on the newly formed sandbars and their roots grow downwards following the lowering water table.

Fremont's Cottonwood

COYOTE WILLOW
Salix exigua
Willow Family (Salicaceae)

Description: Shrub, growing in colonies, generally 6–9' tall with ashy gray stems. Branches reddish and flexible; buds covered by a single scale. Linear leaves ³/₄–4¹/₂" long, generally 10–20 times longer than wide, may have long silky hairs, and leaf margins may be finely toothed. Clusters of separate male and female flowers may form as or after the leaves develop. Fruit is a capsule. RIP.

Late winter–spring.

Comments: *Salix* is the classic Latin name for "willow." The flexible stems were used by Native Americans in basketry and split-willow figurines.

Coyote Willow

NETLEAF HACKBERRY
Celtis reticulata
Elm Family (Ulmaceae)

Description: Small tree, 15-20' tall, with a spreading canopy. Bark veined with corky ridges at maturity. Leaves egg- or lance-shaped, rounded at the base, rough on the surface, toothed along the margin, and typically infested with insect galls. Flowers minute and inconspicuous; spherical fruits reddish to orange or dark red, and fleshy and sweet. RIP, HG.

Midspring–late spring.

Comments: Fruits edible, mostly eaten by mammals. *Reticulata* refers to the intricate "netlike" venation of the leaves; the derivation of *Celtis* is obscure.

Netleaf Hackberry

BLUE FLOWERS

*Bluish flowers often grade into other hues,
so you should also check the pink and
purple flower section.*

UTAH DAISY
Erigeron utahensis
Sunflower Family (Asteraceae)

Description: Perennial, up to 2' high, stems appearing grayish or silvery due to short, stiff hairs. Withered leaves may be present at the base. Lower leaves ³/₈–4" long, narrow, and linear to wider at the tip; upper leaves smaller. Flower heads ¹/₂" wide, solitary or in clusters with 10–40 bluish or white rays surrounding a dense cluster of yellowish disk flowers. Seeds have a double row of bristles. StDS, PJ, Blk.

Spring.

Comments: The type specimen of this species was collected near Kanab, Utah, thus the name *utahensis* (of Utah).

Utah Daisy

Silvery Lupine

SILVERY LUPINE
Lupinus argenteus
Pea Family (Fabaceae)

Description: Perennial, 7–34" tall, the stems and leaf petioles having soft or stiff short hairs. Compound leaves ¹/₂–3" long with 6–9 spatula- or inversely lance-shaped leaflets that have short stiff hairs on both sides or are smooth above. Large flowering stalks bear 15–92 bluish purple flowers, ³/₈–³/₄" long, the upper petal having a central yellow or white spot. Pods may be hairy or smooth and contain 3–6 seeds. StDS, CDS, PJ, SDS.

Mid–late spring.

Comments: *Lupinus* is from Latin *lupus* (wolf), in reference to the plants "wolfing" or taking nourishment from the soil.

Dwarf Lupine

DWARF LUPINE
Lupinus pusillus
Pea Family (Fabaceae)

Description: Annual, up to 9" tall, with long, spreading hairs on the stems and leaf petioles. Leaflets 3–9, inversely lance-shaped, $1/2$–$1^1/2$" long, flat or folded, and smooth above with long soft hairs below. Flower stalk bears 4–38 bluish or bicolored flowers, $1/4$–$1/2$" long, and the upper petal has a yellow spot. Seedpods fairly oval, with constrictions between the seeds. Blk, MDS, SDS, PJ.

Early–late spring.

Comments: *Pusillus* (dwarf) refers to the small stature of these plants. Often grows in sandy soils.

SILVERY SOPHORA
Sophora stenophylla
Pea Family (Fabaceae)

Description: Perennial, 4–16" tall. Lacy leaves alternate, linear to oblong, and covered with dense, soft, silvery hairs. Terminal flowering stalks have 12–39 blue or bluish purple, pea-shaped flowers. Pods have 1–5 seeds and short, stiff hairs lying closely against the pod's surface. SDS, Blk, PJ.

Midspring.

Comments: Herbage and seeds are toxic to livestock if eaten in large quantities. Silvery Sophora colonizes areas by underground horizontal roots.

Silvery Sophora

BLUE FLAX
Linum perenne
Flax Family (Linaceae)

Description: Perennial, from a stout taproot, stems to 2¹/₂'. Basal leaves linear, up to 1¹/₄" long, and in a whorled pattern; upper leaves smaller. Blue or bluish white flowers have a yellowish center and are 1" wide. Five papery petals short-lived, often falling off within a day. Fruit is a small, squat globe. CDS, PJ, MDS.

Midspring–midsummer.

Comments: Originally called *L. lewisii* in honor of western explorer Meriwether Lewis. Cultivated flax, from which linen thread and linseed oil are manufactured, is a close relative.

Blue Flax

ANDERSON'S LARKSPUR
Delphinium andersonii
Buttercup Family (Ranunculaceae)

Description: Perennial, 4–24" tall. Stems are mostly smooth and arise from a basal cluster of leaves; a few leaves may be present along the lower portion of the stem. Leaf blades ³/₈–2³/₈" wide and usually divided 3 times. One to 15 flowers borne along an elongated axis; 5 petal-like sepals bluish, 2 lower petals spreading and broad, the upper one forming a prominent spur. Blk, SDS, PJ.

Midspring.

Comments: *Delphinium* (like a dolphin) refers to the shape of the flower buds. Contain the alkaloid *delphinine*, which is very toxic to livestock. After flowering the toxicity of the alkaloid diminishes.

DIANE ALLEN

Anderson's Larkspur

Dusty Penstemon

DUSTY PENSTEMON
Penstemon comarrhenus
Figwort Family (Scrophulariaceae)

Description: Perennial, 1–4' tall, with smooth stems. Basal leaves inversely lance-shaped, opposite, $^3/_4$-5" long, and the few stem leaves linear and smaller. Flowers pale blue, $^3/_4$–1$^1/_2$" long, and the anther sacs woolly. CDS, PJ.

Midspring–early summer.

Comments: *Penstemon* is from the Greek *pen,* "almost," and *stemon,* "thread," referring to the stamens; only 4 of the 5 stamens produce pollen, so the fifth is almost a stamen.

ORANGE AND RED FLOWERS

*This section contains orange and red flowers
found in the Canyonlands region.*

Butterfly-Weed

BUTTERFLY-WEED
Asclepias tuberosa
Milkweed Family (Asclepiadaceae)

Description: Bushy herbaceous perennial to 3' tall; stout stems covered with small, coarse hairs. Sap is clear. Narrow, short-stemmed leaves lance- to dagger-shaped, and approximately 4" long. Lower leaves alternate, upper leaves may be opposite. Flower clusters with about 25 small-stalked, orange to yellowish red flowers, each with 5 reflexed petals and 5 erect hoods. Spindle-shaped pods, up to 6" long, have small, soft hairs. RIP, PJ.

Late spring–midsummer.

Comments: Roots of Butterfly-Weed are used to treat lung ailments; another common name for this plant is "pleurisy-root." Butterfly-Weed is found in modern herbal teas.

CLARETCUP
Echinocereus triglochidiatus
Cactus Family (Cactaceae)

Description: Few to several hundred stems in compact hemispheric clumps or mounds. Stems mainly cylindrical, up to 1' long and 1–2$\frac{1}{2}$" thick, and with 9 or 10 ribs. Central spines straight or slightly curved, 1–1$\frac{1}{2}$" long, the radial spines smaller. Flowers scarlet and the fruits red at maturity. Blk, CDS, PJ.

Early–midspring.

Comments: *Echinocereus* is from the Greek *echinos* (hedgehog), referring to this plant's resemblance to the animal. *Triglochidiatus* refers to the straight spines arranged in clusters of three. Fruits are edible.

Claretcup

COMMON GLOBEMALLOW
Sphaeralcea coccinea
Mallow Family (Malvaceae)

Description: Perennial, with stems solitary or many from a woody base, 2–18" tall. Leaf blades longer than wide; the 3–5 deep lobes may be again lobed or toothed. Orange to scarlet flowers, 1/2" wide with numerous stamens, borne along an elongated stalk. Rounded capsule contains numerous tiny black seeds. Blk, StDS, CDS, PJ.

Midspring–early summer.

Comments: *Sphaeralcea*, from *sphaira* (globe) and *alcea* (the name of a related genus), refers to the spherical fruits. *Coccinea* (scarlet) refers to the floral color. Sometimes bees of the genus *Diadaysia* can be found in the morning curled up in the flowers.

Common Globemallow

SLENDERLEAF GLOBEMALLOW
Sphaeralcea leptophylla
Mallow Family (Malvaceae)

Description: Perennial, stems few to many, 8–22" tall. Leaf blades 3-lobed, the linear lobes 3/8–1 1/4" long. Stems and leaves with grayish hairs. Flowers orange, 1/2" wide, with numerous stamens. Spherical capsule contains tiny seeds. StDS, Blk, PJ.

Midspring–early summer.

Comments: *Leptophylla* (with slender leaves) describes the lobes on this plant's leaves. The roots of one of the eastern members of the mallow family were once used to make marshmallows.

Slenderleaf Globemallow

Scarlet Gilia

SCARLET GILIA
Gilia aggregata
Phlox Family (Polemoniaceae)

Description: Biennial or perennial, with stems arising from a basal rosette of leaves that are deeply lobed with narrow segments. Stems 40" or taller, and have sticky or white hairs. Stem leaves similar to the basal ones but smaller. Reddish flowers borne in loose clusters; flowers $3/4$–$1^1/2$" long with a long, narrow tube and pointed, flaring lobes. WDS, CDS, PJ, RIP. *Midspring–autumn.*

Comments: *Gilia* is for Filippo Luigi Gilii (1756-1821), a scientist and astronomer. *Aggregata* (clustered) refers to the close arrangement of the flowers. Plants may have a skunklike odor.

CARMINE GILIA
Gilia subnuda
Phlox Family (Polemoniaceae)

Description: Biennial or perennial, 6–20" tall, with a basal rosette of leaves with sticky hairs. Leaves spatula- to egg-shaped, variously lobed, and $3/4$–$3^3/4$" long. Reddish or carmine flowers clustered at the ends of thin stems; corolla tube $3/8$–$3/4$" long and flaring to 5 lobes at the opening. WDS, CDS, PJ.
Late spring–midsummer.

Comments: The sticky hairs tend to catch blowing sand, thus the leaves and stems may have a sandy coating. Also called Sand Gilia.

Carmine Gilia

COMMON PAINTBRUSH
Castilleja chromosa
Figwort Family (Scrophulariaceae)

Description: Perennial, 4–20" tall; stems clustered and with fine hairs. Lower leaves linear or lance-shaped; the upper leaves have 1–3 lobes; all have fine, stiff hairs. Flowerlike bracts reddish and tubular; the cleft calyx lobes have rounded segments. Corolla green and 2-lipped, the upper lip beaklike and the lower lip shorter and 3-toothed. Blk, MDS, CDS, PJ.

Early–midspring.

Comments: *Castilleja* is for Domingo Castillejo, an eighteenth-century Spanish botanist. *Chromosa* (red) describes the color of the flower's bracts. Plants are partially parasitic on the roots of other plants.

Common Paintbrush

ANNUAL PAINTBRUSH
Castilleja exilis
Figwort Family (Scrophulariaceae)

Description: Annual, with erect stems 4–36" tall, the stems having sticky, long, straight hairs. Leaves linear and narrowing to a point. Flowers borne along an elongated stalk, the bracts scarlet for half their length. RIP, HG.

Summer–early autumn.

Comments: Found in wet areas, seeps, springs, wetlands, or along river courses. Flowers resemble a paintbrush dipped in red paint.

Annual Paintbrush

Wyoming Paintbrush

WYOMING PAINTBRUSH
Castilleja linariifolia
Figwort Family (Scrophulariaceae)

Description: Perennial, 8–32". Grasslike or lance-shaped leaves ³/₈–4" long; some leaves have several pairs of narrow lobes. Conspicuous flowers have scarlet bracts with 1–2 pairs of deeply divided lobes that sit below the corolla. The 2-lipped corolla is greenish and rises above the bracts. PJ, RIP, HG.

Late spring–summer.

Comments: State flower of Wyoming, this semi-parasitic paintbrush grows in riparian or moist habitats. *Linariifolia* (with leaves like *Linaria*) refers to the narrow leaves, which resemble those of *Linaria*, another member of the Figwort Family.

SCARLET MONKEYFLOWER
Mimulus eastwoodiae
Figwort Family (Scrophulariaceae)

Description: Perennial, up to 15" tall with stout rounded stems. Leaves opposite; upper leaves dark green, elliptical to broadly lance-shaped, toothed along the margins, deeply veined, and pointed at the tip. Calyx has 5 angular, pointed lobes; the dried calyx may overwinter. Reddish, tubular corolla, 1" long, flares open at the mouth. Flowers 2-lipped, the lips unequal. HG.

Late spring–summer.

Comments: *Mimulus* is from Latin *mimus* (mimic), referring to the flowers mimicking a monkey's face or possibly to the monkeylike resemblance of the plant hanging from alcove ceilings. *Eastwoodiae* is for Alice Eastwood (1859–1953), a curator of botany at the California Academy of Sciences.

Scarlet Monkeyflower

EATON'S PENSTEMON
Penstemon eatonii
Figwort Family (Scrophulariaceae)

Description: Robust perennial, with few to several stems from a short woody base. Plants to 40" tall or more. Basal leaves clustered, smooth, dark green, wavy along the margins, and 1–7" long. Leaf blades broad and narrowed at the base. Red tubular flowers 1–1¹/₂" long, hanging downwards, and may flare open slightly at the tip. Blk, MDS, CDS, PJ.

Midspring–early summer.

Comments: *Penstemon* is from the Greek *pen*, "almost," and *stemon*, "thread," referring to the stamens. *Eatonii* is for David Cady Eaton (1834–1885), an American botanist.

Eaton's Penstemon

Utah Penstemon

UTAH PENSTEMON
Penstemon utahensis
Figwort Family (Scrophulariaceae)

Description: Perennial, with smooth stems, 6–24" tall. Leaves thick and leathery, rounded to obtuse at the tip. Basal leaves ³/₄–4" long, spatula- to broadly inversely lance-shaped. Stem leaves smaller and more lance-shaped. Flowers reddish; corolla tube ¹/₂–³/₄" long, the lobes spreading flat at the opening. MDS, Blk, PJ.

Midspring–early summer.

Comments: *Utahensis* (of Utah) refers to the origin of the type specimen, which was found near Monticello, Utah.

GLOSSARY

Alternate—placed singly along a stem or axis, one after another, usually each successive item on a different side from the previous; often used in reference to the arrangement of leaves on a stem (*see* Opposite).

Annual—a plant completing its life cycle, from seed germination to production of new seeds, within a year, and then dying.

Axil—the area created on the upper side of the angle between a leaf and stem.

Basal—at the base or bottom of; generally used in reference to leaves arranged at the base of the plant.

Biennial—a plant completing its life cycle in two years, and normally not producing flowers during the first year.

Bract—reduced or modified leaf, often associated with flowers.

Bristle—a stiff hair, usually erect or curving away from its attachment point.

Bulb—underground plant part derived from a short, usually rounded, shoot that is covered with scales or leaves.

Calyx—the outer set of flower parts, composed of the sepals, which may be separate or joined together; usually green.

Capsule—a dry fruit that releases seeds through splits or holes.

Cluster—any grouping or close arrangement of individual flowers that is not dense and continuous.

Compound Leaf— a leaf that is divided into two to many leaflets, each of which may look like a complete leaf, but which lacks buds. Compound leaves may have leaflets arranged along an axis like the rays of a feather or radiating from a common point like the fingers on a hand (*see* illustration p. 21).

Corolla—the set of flower parts interior to the calyx and surrounding the stamens, composed of the petals, which may be free or united; often brightly colored.

Deciduous—broad-leaved trees or shrubs that drop their leaves at the end of each growing season, as contrasted with plants that retain the leaves throughout the year (*see* Evergreen).

Disk Flower—small, tubular flowers in the central portion of the flower head of many plants in the Sunflower Family (Asteraceae) (*see* illustration p. 26).

Elliptical (Leaf Shape)—*see* illustration p. 22

Entire (Leaf Margin)—*see* illustration p. 23

Evergreen—plants that bear green leaves throughout the year, as contrasted with plants that lose their leaves at the end of the growing season (*see* Deciduous).

Family—a group of plants having biologically similar features, such as flower anatomy, fruit type, etc.

Flower Head—as used in this guide, a dense and continuous group of flowers, without obvious branches or space between them; used especially in reference to the Sunflower Family (Asteraceae).

Genus—a group of closely related species, such as the genus *Penstemon* encompassing the penstemons (*see* Specific Epithet).

Herbaceous—a term that refers to any nonwoody plant; often reserved for wildflowers.

Hood—curving or folded, petal-like structures interior to the petals and exterior to the stamens in milkweed (Asclepiadaceae) flowers; since most milkweeds have reflexed petals, the hoods are typically the most prominent feature of the flowers.

Inflorescence—generally a cluster of flowers, although there are many terms to specifically describe the arrangement of flowers on the plant.

Involucre—a distinct series of bracts or leaves that subtend a flower or cluster of flowers. Often used in the description of the Sunflower Family (Asteraceae) flower heads.

Keel—a sharp lengthwise fold or ridge, referring particularly to the two fused petals forming the lower lip in many flowers of the Pea Family (Fabaceae).

Lance (Leaf Shape)—*see* illustration p. 22

Leaflet—a distinct, leaflike segment of a compound leaf.

Linear (Leaf Shape)—*see* illustration p. 22

Lobe—a segment of an incompletely divided plant part, typically rounded; often used in reference to the leaves.

Midrib—the central or main vein of a leaf.

Node—the region of the stem where one or more leaves are attached. Buds are commonly borne at the node, in the axils of the leaves.

Nutlet—a descriptive term for small nutlike fruits. Used to describe the separate lobes of a mature ovary in the Borage and Mint families.

Oblong (Leaf Shape)—*see* illustration p. 22

Opposite—paired directly across from one another along a stem or axis (*see* Alternate).

Ovary—the portion of the flower where the seeds develop, usually a swollen area below the style (if present) and stigma.

Pappus—in the Sunflower Family (Asteraceae) the modified limb of the calyx is the pappus, and consists of a crown of bristles, hairs, or scales at the top of the seed.

Parallel—side by side, approximately the same distance apart for the entire length; often used in reference to veins or edges of leaves.

Perennial—a plant that normally lives for three or more years.

Petal—component part of the corolla, often the most brightly colored and visible part of the flower.

Petiole—the stalk of a leaf. The length of the petiole may be used in leaf descriptions.

Pinnate—a compound leaf, like many of the Pea Family (Fabaceae) members, where smaller leaflets are arranged along either side of a common axis.

Pistil—the seed-producing, or female, part of a flower, consisting of the ovary, style (if present), and stigma; a flower may have one to several separate pistils.

Pollen—tiny, often powdery male reproductive cells formed in the stamens and typically necessary for seed production.

Ray Flower—flower in the Sunflower Family (Asteraceae) with a single, strap-shaped corolla, resembling one flower petal; several to many ray flowers may surround the disk flowers in a flower head, or in some species such as dandelions, the flower heads may be composed entirely of ray flowers (*see* illustration p. 26).

Rosette—a dense cluster of basal leaves from a common underground part, often in a flattened, circular arrangement.

Scale—any thin, membranous body that somewhat resembles the scales of fish or reptiles.

Sepal—component part of the calyx; typically green but sometimes enlarged and brightly colored.

Shrub—a perennial woody plant of relatively low height, and typically with several stems arising from or near the ground.

Simple Leaf—a leaf that has a single leaflike blade, although this may be lobed or divided.

Spatula (Leaf Shape)—*see* illustration p.22

Specific Epithet—the second portion of a scientific name, identifying a particular species; for instance in Four-Wing Saltbush, *Atriplex canescens*, the specific epithet is *"canescens."*

Spike—an elongate, unbranched cluster of stalkless or nearly stalkless flowers.

Stalk—as used here, the stem supporting the leaf, flower, or flower cluster.

Stalkless—lacking a stalk; a stalkless leaf is attached directly to the stem at the leaf base.

Stamen—the male unit of a flower, which produces the pollen; typically consisting of a long filament with a pollen-producing tip.

Standard—the usually erect, spreading upper petal in many flowers of the Pea Family (Fabaceae).

Stigma—portion of the pistil receptive to pollination; usually at the top of the style, and often appearing fuzzy or sticky.

Style—the portion of the pistil between the ovary and the stigma; typically a slender stalk.

Subtend—situated below or beneath, often encasing or enclosing something.

Toothed—bearing teeth, or sharply angled projections, along the edge.

Variety—a group of plants within a species that has a distinct range, habitat, structure.

Whorl—three or more parts attached at the same point along a stem or axis and often surrounding the stem.

Wings—the two side petals flanking the keel in many flowers of the Pea Family (Fabaceae).

SELECTED REFERENCES

Coffey, Timothy. 1993. *The History and Folklore of North American Wildflowers.* New York: Facts-on-File.

Comstock, Jonathan P. and James R. Ehleringer. 1992. *Plant Adaptation in the Great Basin and Colorado Plateau.* Great Basin Naturalist 52(3): 195-215.

Dunmire, William W. and Gail D. Tierney. 1995. *Wild Plants of the Pueblo Province: Exploring Ancient and Enduring Uses.* Santa Fe: Museum of New Mexico Press.

Elmore, Francis H. 1976. *Shrubs and Trees of the Southwest Uplands.* Globe, Ariz.: Southwest Parks and Monuments Association.

Harrington, H. D. and L. W. Durrell. 1979. *How to Identify Plants.* 1957. Reprint, Athens: University of Ohio Press, Swallow Press.

Heil, Kenneth D., J. Mark Porter, Rich Fleming, and William H. Romme. 1993. *Vascular Flora and Vegetation of Capitol Reef National Park, Utah.* United States Department of the Interior National Park Service Technical Report NPS/NAUCARE/NRTR 93/01.

Hitchcock, C. Leo and Arthur Cronquist. 1973. *Flora of the Pacific Northwest.* Seattle: University of Washington Press.

Howe, Henry F. and Lynn C. Westley. 1988. *Ecological Relationships of Plants and Animals.* New York: Oxford University Press.

Kricher, John C. and Gordon Morrison. 1993. *A Field Guide to the Ecology of Western Forests.* Boston: Houghton Mifflin.

Leake, Dorothy Van Dyke, John B. Leake, and Marcelotte Leake Roeder. 1993. *Desert and Mountain Plants of the Southwest.* Norman: University of Oklahoma Press.

Louw, Gideon and Mary Seely. 1982. *Ecology of Desert Organisms.* London: William Clowes.

MacMahon, James. 1985. *Deserts.* Audubon Society Nature Guide. New York: Alfred A. Knopf.

Proctor, Michael and Peter Yeo. 1972. *The Pollination of Flowers.* New York: Taplinger Publishing.

Rahm, David A. 1974. *Reading the Rocks: A Guide to the Geologic Secrets of Canyons, Mesas and Buttes of the American Southwest.* San Francisco: Sierra Club Books.

Santillo, Humbart. 1985. *Natural Healing with Herbs.* Prescott Valley, Ariz.: Hohm Press.

Sounders, Charles F. 1933. *Western Wild Flowers and Their Stories.* Garden City, N.Y.: Doubleday, Doran.

Tweit, Susan J. 1992. *The Great Southwest Nature Factbook.* Seattle: Alaska Northwest Books.

Welsh, Stanley L., N. Duane Atwood, Sherel Goodrich, and Larry C. Higgins. 1993. *A Utah Flora.* Provo, Utah: Brigham Young University.

Wormwood, Valerie A. 1991. *The Complete Book of Essential Oils and Aromatherapy.* San Rafael, Calif.: New World Library.

Zwinger, Ann H. 1989. *The Mysterious Lands: A Naturalist Explores the Four Great Deserts of the Southwest.* Tucson: University of Arizona Press.

*I*NDEX

About the Author

Damian Fagan is a naturalist residing in the canyon country of southeastern Utah with his wife, Raven, and daughter, Luna Sierra. He completed a B.S. in Botany from the University of Washington in 1982, then moved to Moab, Utah, to work for the National Park Service as a seasonal park ranger. In 1991 he founded BUTEO Wildlife Consultants, specializing in population inventories and project clearances on the avian fauna of the Colorado Plateau, for private organizations and government agencies. When not out birding, he writes natural history articles and photographs the inhabitants of the Canyonlands region.

Canyonlands Natural History Association

The Canyonlands Natural History Association (CNHA) is a nonprofit organization that provides educational materials that aid in the understanding and appreciation of the region. All proceeds support interpretive and scientific programs conducted by the National Park Service, U.S.D.A. Forest Service, and Bureau of Land Management in the canyon country of southeastern Utah. To contact CNHA, call (800) 840-8978; publications and maps are available by mail.

get
FALCON GUIDED

FALCON has **FALCON** GUIDES® for hiking, mountain biking, rock climbing, walking, scenic driving, fishing, rockhounding, paddling, birding, wildlife viewing, and camping. Here are a few titles currently available, but this list grows every year. If you would like a free catalog with a complete list of available titles, call FALCON at the toll-free number at the bottom of this page.

SCENIC DRIVING GUIDES

Scenic Driving Alaska and the Yukon
Scenic Driving Arizona
Scenic Driving the Beartooth Highway
Scenic Driving California
Scenic Driving Colorado
Scenic Driving Florida
Scenic Driving Georgia
Scenic Driving Hawaii
Scenic Driving Idaho
Scenic Driving Michigan
Scenic Driving Minnesota
Scenic Driving Montana
Scenic Driving New England
Scenic Driving New Mexico
Scenic Driving North Carolina
Scenic Driving Oregon
Scenic Driving the Ozarks including the
    Ouchita Mountains
Scenic Driving Texas
Scenic Driving Utah
Scenic Driving Washington
Scenic Driving Wisconsin
Scenic Driving Wyoming
Back Country Byways
National Forest Scenic Byways
National Forest Scenic Byways II

Traveling California's Gold Rush Country
Traveler's Guide to the Lewis & Clark Trail
Traveling the Oregon Trail
Traveler's Guide to the Pony Express Trail

WILDLIFE VIEWING GUIDES

Alaska Wildlife Viewing Guide
Arizona Wildlife Viewing Guide
California Wildlife Viewing Guide
Colorado Wildlife Viewing Guide
Florida Wildlife Viewing Guide
Idaho Wildlife Viewing Guide
Indiana Wildlife Vewing Guide
Iowa Wildlife Viewing Guide
Kentucky Wildlife Viewing Guide
Massachusetts Wildlife Viewing Guide
Montana Wildlife Viewing Guide
Nebraska Wildlife Viewing Guide
Nevada Wildlife Viewing Guide
New Hampshire Wildlife Viewing Guide
New Jersey Wildlife Viewing Guide
New Mexico Wildlife Viewing Guide
New York Wildlife Viewing Guide
North Carolina Wildlife Viewing Guide
North Dakota Wildlife Viewing Guide

■ *To order any of these books, check with your local bookseller
or call FALCON® at **1-800-582-2665***

FALCON®

Visit us on the world wide web at:
http://www.falconguide.com

get
FALCONGUIDED

BIRDING GUIDES
Birding Arizona
Birding Minnesota
Birder's Guide to Montana
Birding Texas
Birding Utah

FIELD GUIDES
Bitterroot: Montana State Flower
Canyonlands Wildflowers
Great Lakes Berry Book
New England Berry Book
Plants of Arizona
Rare Plants of Colorado
Rocky Mountain Berry Book
Tallgrass Prairie Wildflowers
Wildflowers of Southwestern Utah
Willow Bark and Rosehips

FISHING GUIDES
Fishing Alaska
Fishing Beartooths
Fishing Maine
Fishing Michigan
Fishing Montana
Fishing Yellowstone

HOW TO GUIDES
Bear Aware
Leave No Trace
Mountain Lion Alert
Wilderness First Aid

PADDLING GUIDES
Floater's Guide to Colorado
Floater's Guide to Missouri
Floater's Guide to Montana
Paddling Okefenokee Swamp
Paddling Oregon
Paddling Yellowstone

ROCK CLIMBING GUIDES
Rock Climbing Colorado
Rock Climbing Montana
Rock Climbing New Mexico & Texas

ROCKHOUNDING GUIDES
Rockhounding Arizona
Rockhound's Guide to California
Rockhound's Guide to Colorado
Rockhounding Montana
Rockhounding Nevada
Rockhound's Guide to New Mexico
Rockhounding Texas
Rockhounding Utah
Rockhounding Wyoming

MORE GUIDEBOOKS
Backcountry Horseman's Guide to
    Washington
Camping California's National Forests
Exploring Canyonlands &
    Arches National Parks
Recreation Guide to Washington
    National Forests

Trail Riding Western Montana
Wild Country Companion
Wild Montana
Wild Utah

WALKING
Walking Colorado Springs
Walking Portland
Walking St. Louis

■ *To order any of these books, check with your local bookseller*
or call FALCON at **1-800-582-2665**
Visit us on the world wide web at:
http://www.falconguide.com

FALCON®

Hiking the National Parks

The national parks have some of the very best hiking in the world, and just because it's a national park doesn't mean it's crowded. In many parks, the roads are clogged with traffic, but the trails are nearly devoid of people.

As part of the **FALCON** GUIDES series, Falcon plans to publish a complete set of hiking guides to every national park with a substantial trail system. If your favorite park isn't on the following list of books currently available, you can plan on it being available soon. Each book comprehensively covers the trails in the parks and includes the necessary trip planning information on access, regulations, weather, etc., to help you put together a memorable adventure.

AVAILABLE NOW:
Hiking Big Bend National Park
Hiking California's Desert Parks (includes Death Valley and Joshua Tree national parks, Mojave National Preserve, and Anza-Borrego State Park)
Hiking Canyonlands & Arches National Parks
Hiking Carlsbad Caverns & Guadalupe Mountains National Parks
Hiking The Columbia River Gorge
Hiking Glacier & Waterton Lakes National Parks
Hiking Grand Canyon National Park
Hiking Great Basin
Hiking North Cascades
Hiking Olympic National Park
Hiking Yellowstone National Park
Hiking South Dakota's Black Hills Country (includes Wind Cave, Badlands and Mount Rushmore national parks, and Custer State Park)
Hiking Zion & Bryce Canyon National Parks

COMING SOON: Redwoods, Glen Canyon/Escalante, Grand Teton, and Rocky Mountain

ALSO AVAILABLE: 26 state-wide hiking guides

TO ORDER:
Check with your local bookseller or
call Falcon at **1-800-582-2665** FALCON®

WILDERNESS FIRST AID

By Dr. Gilbert Preston M.D.
Enjoy the outdoors and face the inherent risks with confidence. By reading this easy-to-follow first-aid text, all outdoor enthusiasts can pack a little extra peace of mind on their next adventure. *Wilderness First Aid* offers expert medical advice for dealing with outdoor emergencies beyond the reach of 911. It easily fits in most backcountry first-aid kits.

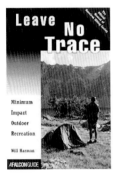

LEAVE NO TRACE

by Will Harmon
The concept of "leave no trace" seems simple, but it actually gets fairly complicated. This handy quick-reference guidebook includes all the newest information on this growing and all-important subject. This book is written to help the outdoor enthusiast make the hundreds of decisions necessary to protect the natural landscape and still have an enjoyable wilderness experience. Part of the proceeds from the sale of this book go to continue leave-no-trace education efforts. The Official Manual of American Hiking Society.

BEAR AWARE

by Bill Schneider
It's hardly news that Yellowstone is good habitat for both grizzly and black bears. Hiking in bear country can be very safe if hikers follow the guidelines summarized in this small, "packable" book. Extensively reviewed by bear experts, the book contains the latest information on the intriguing science of bear-human interactions. *Bear Aware* can not only make your hike safer, but it can help you avoid the fear of bears that can take the edge off your trip.

MOUNTAIN LION ALERT

By Steve Torres
Recent mountain lion attacks in California received national attention. Although infrequent, these and other lion attacks raise concern for public safety. *Mountain Lion Alert* contains helpful advice for mountain bikers, trail runners, horse riders, pet owners, and suburban landowners on how to reduce the chances of mountain lion-human conflicts.

To order these titles or to find out more about this new series of books, call FALCON® at **1-800-582-2665.**